WHERE THE SKY ENDS

WHERE THE SKY ENDS

A Memoir of Alcohol and Family

M. G. STEPHENS

INFORMATION & EDUCATIONAL SERVICES

Hazelden
Center City, Minnesota 55012-0176

1-800-328-0094
1-651-213-4590 (Fax)
www.hazelden.org

Library of Congress Cataloging-in-Publication Data
Stephens, Michael Gregory.
    Where the sky ends : a memoir of alcohol and family /
M. G. Stephens.
    p. cm.
    ISBN 1-56838-339-8
    1. Stephens, Michael Gregory. 2. Recovering alcoholics—
United States Biography. 3. Authors, American—20th century
Biography. 4. Alcoholics—United States—Family relationships.
5. Alcoholism—United States. I. Title.
HV5293.S74A3   1999
362.292'092—dc21
[B]   99-34358
                                                           CIP

03 02 01 00 99 6 5 4 3 2 1

Cover design by David Spohn
Interior design by Nora Koch/Gravel Pit Publications
Typesetting by Nora Koch/Gravel Pit Publications

This book is dedicated to Susan, with love

"... to trust and to celebrate what is constant—birth, struggle, and death are constant, and so is love, though we may not always think so—and to apprehend the nature of change, to be able and willing to change."

—James Baldwin

"As to me I know of nothing else but miracles"

—Walt Whitman

CONTENTS

Acknowledgments

"Farewell to the Chief" appeared in *The American Scholar;* "Prayer for My Father" appeared in *Manoa;* "Who You Are" in *Crazyhorse;* "The Gratitude" in *Hanging Loose;* "Clearwater Blues" in *Witness;* "Meditation on the Harp" in *Speak;* and "The Amends" in *Notre Dame Review.* "Meditation on the Harp" was reprinted in *The Art of the Essay 1999.*

The author wishes to thank all the editors of these journals for their support, especially Joseph Epstein, Frank Stewart, Dennis Vannatta, Bob Hershon, Peter Stine, Dan Rolleri, Bill O'Rourke, and Phillip Lopate.

I wish to thank several people without whose help I could not have completed this book: my editor Steve Lehman and my agent Esmond Harmsworth. I also want to thank Jenny Kimball for introducing my work to Esmond. Richard Hoffman, writer, friend, and fellow traveler, read the manuscript and made excellent suggestions. Ivan Gold generously read an earlier version too. Kate Kjorlien copyedited the manuscript with care and understanding for its narrative voice.

Finally, I need to build a city of gratitude to Susan Wolan who acted as a developmental editor on the manuscript, from earliest versions until the present; no one read more drafts of this work than she did nor had more good advice concerning the manuscript; she believed in this book even when I did not, and encouraged me not to give up before the miracle.

I.

1

The Dead

After Joe parks the van in the lot in front of the funeral parlor—across the street from Saint Cecilia's church—we step into the Druid Chapel, where my father is laid out. It is a modest funeral parlor, and we find the chapel easily; we simply follow the noise. The chapel is not filled up yet, but already the relatives all talk at once, creating a din. I see my mother in the front of the room surrounded by her two oldest sons, Jimmy and Peter; my three sisters—Kaitlin, Rosemary, and Peggy—are sitting in chairs right in front of my mother. Some of them nod or wave to us. Others go on talking. I see my parents' Floridian friends, men and women with wrinkled, robust, sunshined skin.

Joe, Brendan, and Tommy move to the front of the room, first to look at their father laid out, then to greet their siblings and finally, their mother. I hang back. If I smoked, I'd go outside for one right now. But I gave it up a few years earlier. Instead, I say hello to some cousins and nephews. I play the uncle or the long-lost cousin. I say hello; I shake hands. I look to the front of the room, where my father is in repose, and think that I should go forward, that I should make my obligatory kneeling in front of the coffin to pray. But something holds me back. Well, it is not something; it is fear. Death scares me, though I am too cowardly to admit that to anyone.

But, of course, my mother notices.

She comes from the front of the room with one of her old friends from Florida. As she walks toward me, stopping to speak to different people, I look to the coffin once again. But once again I freeze, unable to go forward to say a prayer. Although I see this tiny version of my mighty old man in the front of the room, no odor of his past escapes from him. Instead, the room's pervasive odors are ones of floral life and rot, wreaths of flowers everywhere in different states of aliveness or decay.

When he was alive, my father smelled of work and sweat and beer on the breath. He smelled of belt leather from the strap that he whacked you with at the drop of a dime. He did not wear deodorant—why, I am not sure—though he bathed every morning. Yet by the end of the day, his odor, from working all day on the docks, was overripe. As they say in the Old Country, "He had a hum coming off himself." He did not smoke, so I do not associate the smell of tobacco with him, but rather with my mother and her Salem cigarettes. He liked onions with smelly cheeses (Gorgonzola comes to mind), and he washed them down with beer, so that he reeked of yeasty and ripe ferment. But even formaldehyde was an odor not incompatible with this man.

Once again I think about going up to the coffin to bid farewell to my father. As if on cue, my mother appears in front of me, chatting with some distant relative or friend.

She says, "Michael gets queasy at funerals."

"No, I don't," I say, but she does not hear.

"Hello, dear," she says, then pecks a kiss on my cheek. "Are you all right?"

"I'm fine, Ma," I say, but I am not. It all reminds me of when I was a young boy and was picked to put a crown of lilac on the statue of the Blessed Mother in May. But I got nauseous from the heat and I nearly passed out. Some girl in the class was chosen at the last minute to fill in for me. While the ceremony went on, an usher made me sit on the curb, tucking my head between my legs as he pushed on the back of my neck, supposedly to stop the nausea. Instead, he brought it on, and I threw up on a brand-new Pontiac four-door sedan parked in front of the church's rectory.

My mother turns back to her friend, back to her endless story, this time about her late husband. It is almost as if her verbal tale and the thoughts in my head coincide—I had been just thinking these very thoughts—because then she says, "His house burnt to the ground." She can mean no one but my father because I don't know of anyone else whose home burnt down.

My mother is unusually cheerful this morning, but then again she and my father, in their later years, enjoyed going to funerals. Of course, too, she saw my father's deterioration and suffering, especially during the last two years of his life. Death, I need to remember, is also a tender mercy, releasing someone from distress and pain.

Under my mother's wrinkled face, I still see a young girl, though, so that equating her with dying is still not easy. She is very much a part of the living.

"Yes," she says, "his house burnt to the ground."

"He lived in a house?" the other woman asks.

"Well, no," my mother says, looking at the woman as if she were crazy. "He lived in an apartment building."

"But you said 'house,' Rose."

Yet New Yorkers, particularly those in Manhattan, often refer to their apartments as houses. This tells me immediately that the woman my mother speaks to is a friend and not a relative, because all of our relatives come from the New York area, and they understand these peculiarities of speech.

"It burnt down," she says.

Once again I recall her telling us children the reason for our father's Christmastime rages. His house burnt to the ground during that holiday season.

I always wanted to ask my mother what made my father so angry and miserable the rest of the year, but I did not.

But his own home burning to the ground on Christmas Day certainly would explain my father's peculiar rages toward his children, often for no reason at all, particularly during the holidays. Or maybe, I imagine, his own father killed my father's mother, and that is why my father, a witness to it, got so nuts with his own children. Sometimes I worry that my grandfather killed his wife, Annie Hopkins. But then I catch myself and say that I am overdramatizing what really are pedestrian lives, people so marginal that drama of any kind never really touched them. They are the salt of the earth, the toilers, and perhaps a Christian god would reward them in the afterlife, but no one was going to give a damn about them when they were alive.

I stop all this reflecting, this endless thinking about the past, and I drill my eyes to the front of the chapel where my father is laid out in his casket. But, once again, something brings me back to the past.

The woman speaking to my mother turns out to be a

Hopkins relative, and she comes over to say hello to me. I have discovered, in the last few years, that Hopkinses like to meet me because I look so much like their own kin, which makes sense, considering that I am one of their kin too. Only I am a long-lost kin, someone they never knew until that moment.

After the usual condolences, she seems to pick up the story of my father, the one that has been running in my head, and then the one my mother introduced, about the fire in his home. My father was five years old when his mother died, and he was set adrift in a scary world because his own father was too drunk to take care of him. That was when the rich uncles from New Jersey stepped in and took my father to Asbury Park where he learned to swim and live a life without a mother. But it does not take a Charles Dickens to realize that a motherless child, like the blues song wails, has a hard time. The man my father became—rough, abrasive, two-fisted, bull-necked, swaggering—was the result of having no mother. It was his camouflage for surviving the horror his life became at the age of five.

The Druid Chapel percolates with life, even if my father, the focal point, is still. Various members of my family roam about the room, saying hello to friends and other relatives. I remain in the back of the chapel, talking to more-distant friends and relatives, as if I do not belong up front with the primary mourners, my brothers and sisters and my mother. I need to get my bearings. At least that is what I tell myself, procrastinating that journey from the back of the chapel to the front. Funerals suck the breath out of me; they are not in my nature. I would not bother with such things as an open casket. My desire is for something quite simple and bare, a cremation, a quiet service afterward, maybe a few songs, a few poems, some passages from a favorite book, perhaps a goofy, off-center jazz rendition of a standard by Thelonious Monk on the sound system. But this is not my end but my father's. If these were not his wishes, then they are my mother's.

The breathless sensation overtakes me. It is what I imagine an asthma attack to be like. I blow my nose, trying to release the bubble in my head. My ears pop, a residual of jet travel, even days later. I sniff, I sniffle. I blow my nose again. People come over to shake my hand, put a hand on my shoulder, offer their condolences. This seems odd to me because I have never been close to my father in my life. True, I have been obsessed by him. I have portrayed terribly comic fathers in my writing since I was a young man. But I have had no formal connection to this ghost in the front of the room since I was a boy. Still, my role in this drama cannot be denied. I am my father's son—one of his many sons, at least. Yet who looks more like the old man than I? Forget about genetic cloning. I not only look like my father, I move like him, behave like him, probably even think like him. Didn't he hate his father too? And didn't he leave Georgetown University to come home to Brooklyn to take care of his ailing father? And yet, when did I take care of him?

I may not be prepared to put the past to rest but, standing in the chapel, I am prepared to put it in perspective. I may not be ready yet to walk to the front of the room, kneel

8

in front of the coffin, and say a prayer for the repose of his soul. But I am prepared to acknowledge that he was not all bad. Cause and effect worked to make him such a pernicious father because his own father had been so negligent and spiteful too. As for his mother, I could fill the back of a matchbook with the information I have about her, my own grandmother.

She came from rural County Mayo in Ireland, and her name was Annie Hopkins. One of my father's cousins, only two years earlier, came over to me and said, "If you ever wonder where you got all your brains, they come from Annie Hopkins."

It was she, Annie, who helped two of her brothers come to America, and they did well in the taxi industry, getting rich in Hell's Kitchen and then moving out to the then rural world of Asbury Park, New Jersey. I remember almost nothing about these two old gents except one visit we paid them as children. To me, this was odd because these were the people who raised my father when his own drunken father disappeared into an alcoholic haze. We were taken, during our one visit to the Hopkinses of New Jersey, to their club pool. My father's skin was as fair as the proverbial young maiden's of folklore, and almost immediately he began to get bright red and had to leave the pool area. One of his ancient Irish uncles laughed.

"Stewart's [the name all his relatives called my father to distinguish him from his father, the other James] got skin like his mother," he said.

I believe that is the only detail I had ever heard about my paternal grandmother until my father's cousin told me, two years earlier, that I got my brains from Annie Hopkins. Yet it is hard to imagine a woman looking like my father with his large head, big nose, gigantic ears, and jutting chin. I know so little about my father; I know even less about his mother. She came from rural Ireland, was a schoolteacher, had fair skin, and, no doubt, was smart. It was she who first came to America. Her brothers followed her. I suppose that what I know about my grandfather is equally scant. He was a peasant from County Clare. He drove taxicabs and trucks and worked, in his last years, in the Brooklyn Navy Yard. His death certificate lists cirrhosis of the liver as the cause of death. That tells me he was a big drinker. When I examined Irish papers about him a few years ago, I discovered that he lied about his age. In America, he appeared to be fifteen years younger than he was.

These two unlikely people—a rural schoolteacher and a peasant farmer (possibly illiterate)—met in Brooklyn and married. They married in the same church, Saint Gregory's, that my father was baptized in and my own parents, too, were married in years later. It is located in what is now called Crown Heights, a tense neighborhood today that is co-inhabited by Orthodox Jews and West Indian blacks. My two first names, Michael and Gregory, come from these two parishes in Brooklyn.

But why dwell on any of this now? I have become phobic about seeing my father in the coffin.

"Haven't you paid your respects yet?" Peter asks.

"I'll go in a minute," I say.

"Come on," my mother says. "It will take a minute."

I feel like a little kid being prodded by his mother and

older brother. They leave to speak to other mourners, and I hang back once more. But then suddenly I am moving. I am walking. I nod hello to relatives and friends. I'm going to the front of the chapel where the coffin is. As I walk toward my father, I am thinking about his mother. I have heard too many cockamamie stories about how she died. Some told of her dying from stomach cancer. Others that she died in that Christmas fire. Sometimes, as I said, I think that she was murdered. But perhaps that is the writer in me speaking, not the son or grandson being dutiful and loyal to her memory or, in my case, my lack of memory concerning her.

As I walk to the casket I am filled with the feeling that the world has slowed down, is as thick and gooey as my Irish grandmother's pancakes were, and that is why it takes me so long to get from the back of the chapel to the front. I have been walking for hours, it seems. I have walked for hours to reach my father. Yet I don't know my father at all. I thought he was a big man. But clearly his tiny casket reveals that he was not; he was quite small in the end, no matter how large he loomed in my life. Death custom-fits him to this half-pint coffin. Yet how appropriate, I think, walking up there to the front of the room, that my father is laid out in the Druid Chapel. I often thought of him as being more pagan than Christian. Part of that feeling came from his look: he never looked like a typical Irishman, and because our name does not sound particularly Irish, people thought that my father was not Irish. Really, it was only in old age that he began to latch on to the sentimental values of the Irish-Americans, the green soup and the stupid green plastic derbies, the jukebox filled with bogus songs by the Clancys. In his heyday, my father could not have cared less about all that Paddy nonsense. Give him a good bar to drink in and that's all he wanted.

He preferred the dives on Forty-ninth Street, going from the piers to Times Square. When we were children, he took many of us to work, and later we ate cheesecake at a table while the old man stood at the bar knocking back shots with Jack Dempsey himself, the legendary former heavyweight boxing champion and the proprietor of the joint. Dempsey even came over and messed up the hair on my brother Peter's head with his inhumanly large hand. Gangsters, loan sharks, numbers runners, cops, firemen, customs officials from the pier, they all knew my father as a swell guy. Too bad their dreamy drunken image of him did not coincide with our own because, invariably, on the Long Island railroad train going back toward Mineola and home, he'd whack one of us with his own overly large hand and threaten to torture us to death if we did not behave.

Sometimes the familiar faces are really strangers; sometimes the strangers are long-lost relations. I say hello to people whom I would not ordinarily speak to. I wouldn't speak to them not out of snobbery but ignorance; I don't know who they are. If I think they are my parents' friends, I discover that they are distant relations, usually on my father's side, because I rarely got to meet his relatives, most of them from Ireland. Or I mistake a face for a Drew, McCann, Stephens, or Hopkins, the names of our family tree, only to find out that I am speaking with a Florida friend of my father's or mother's or both. This woman comes over to say hello and I return the greeting. I am not sure where she fits in the scheme of things, and I don't ask.

"How are you, Michael?" she asks.

"I'm fine," I lie.

"Good," this old coot says.

"Yes," I answer.

"And your family?"

"They are well too."

"Let's see," she says, "you married the girl from Poland?"

"Korea," I answer.

"That's right," she says. "Korea. How is the dear thing?"

"The dear thing is fine," I say.

She looks at me strangely, for it is all right for her to call my wife a dear thing, but when I say it back, it reminds her just how strange her remark is. So I move on. I move forward, toward the front of the room and my dead father.

"This is my brother Michael," Peter says, introducing me to one of my parents' Florida friends.

"Hi," I say.

"I'm sorry," the woman says.

"Yeah, well," I say, but do not finish my remark.

"She's a friend of Bill," Peter says.

"Bill?" I ask.

"You know," Peter says, getting annoyed. "Bill W."

"Oh, Bill W.," I say. I turn to her. "Me, I'm a friend of Dr. Bob."

The woman laughs, all of us familiar with the shorthand introductions of alcoholics in recovery.

Peter takes her by the elbow and moves away, and so I

must move on once more. I see my father's big nose protruding from over the lip of the coffin, but at this angle his face is invisible to me.

"That's Michael," my sister Kaitlin says, pointing to me, as a large, old woman stands over her. "You know, from Manhattan."

"Oh, the big-shot writer, yes," the lady says and smiles absently at me.

I can't prolong this visit further. I stand in front of my father. I stand and look at him. Then I turn away, looking around the room as if I lost someone or something. I look back, and my heart sinks into my stomach. I feel a slight wave of nausea push through me. I swallow but have no saliva in my mouth. Suddenly the funeral parlor chapel seems oppressively hot and airless. I look at my father in repose. I stand in front of the coffin, I look down, and then I kneel. I even bless myself, making the sign of the cross, something I have not done since I was a teenager.

First sight of my father: his immigrant face so un-American but not typically Irish either. Looking at him, I see how non-Europeans see all Europeans as the same. He has the face of a European peasant. It is the face of someone who might just as easily be at home in Croatia or Poland as in the British Isles or Ireland. Though his frame had shrunk to less than half its adult size, his face maintained its enormity. In fact, shrinking of the body had made his face appear even larger than it was. I see the big nose, the jug ears, the big chin, bushy eyebrows, hair still peppered with blackness, a mole above his right eye. He is not too wrinkled, not as much as my mother is. He smiles. It is a Mona Lisa smile, full of irony, as if he has had the last laugh. Perhaps he has.

It is not tears that want to pour out of me. Instead, I am twitching and bursting from my skin. I do not hate this man; I love him, even if I have spent most of my life not liking him. But what is it I did not like? Well, I might start with his attitude. He had a very street attitude, full of ill will and what is called in the boxing game "bad intentions." I probably need to throw in his violence, his verbal abuse, his stubbornness, his general demeanor, which is to say, working-class, resentful, bullying. In too many respects, though, I am looking at myself. I stare at myself in the coffin. But that is not what terrifies me. I am scared when I think of how incapable he and I both were of expressing our feelings to each other.

As I kneel in front of my father, looking at his placid, cold face, I do not want to shout and curse the way Marlon Brando did in *Last Tango in Paris,* though coming from the back of the chapel to the front, I thought perhaps that is what I would do. But I will not. Mourning becomes Electra but not me. I am not dutiful, not suppliant enough. The cornerstone of my relationship with my father was founded on irresolution. Without a beginning, middle, or end, there is no closure, only the open wounds. I have these unpatriotic thoughts of leaving the dead behind; no wonder the military didn't want me and kicked me out after one day of boot camp. But I am enough of an American to know that you do not leave your dead or wounded behind; that is rule number one. I will kneel here for as long as it takes to make some kind of resolution with my father. Failing that, I will kneel here, doing nothing but experiencing these feelings that seem to suffocate and strangle me.

I repeat a mantra that I have chanted since arriving in Florida. It goes something like this: This is my father. No matter what I thought of him or what I now think of him, no matter how bad our relationship had been, this is my father, and now he is dead. He seems neither sick enough nor old enough to be dead. He never smoked, he walked everywhere, and he should have been alive—and well—to enjoy more of his old age. He had grandchildren to meet. Walks to take. Conversations with friends that had not been completed. There were newspapers to be read. Television shows to watch, like his and my mother's favorite, *Laverne and Shirley.* There were arguments to have. Resentments to foment. Grudges to cherish. People to holler at. Curses to be made.

As I kneel in front of my father, I recall one of the few photographs that survives my own childhood. I am four years old. We have just moved from Brooklyn to Williston Park. I stand on the stoop of our new house. I wear what amounts to a uniform: Hopalong Cassidy cowboy boots given to me on my fourth birthday by Aunt Katherine Taylor, a beat-up flannel shirt, and overly large dungarees with a cowboy belt—obviously hand-me-downs from my older brothers because none of it fits right. My hair is mussed up and uncombed. I am so shy that I cannot, for the life of me, look into the camera, and I cannot remember who felt that I was important enough to warrant my own portrait without the rest of the family present. My nose is too large on my face; my ears are like jugs; I have an ironic, Mona Lisa–like smile. (It is a smile that is not unlike the one on the corpse in front of me.) I am not a tough guy like my father and my two older brothers; I am as vulnerable as a newborn child. I don't know anyone yet. My shyness is such that I can't imagine ever meeting any new friends. My underwear is dirty and it itches because it is a hot, sticky day in July. Bees scare me. Bugs scare me. People scare me. Thunder scares me. Even frogs scare me.

Perhaps that is why one of my older brothers puts a frog down my shirt, turning the fear into terror. My mother is too busy to attend to me. She has five children with another on the way. Where is my father? I want my father here but he is at work. I want my father to kiss my cheek and tell me that everything is going to be all right. But my father never says that everything is going to be all right. *Be a man,* he says. *Act tough. Don't be a sissy. Stand up for yourself.* I cry.

Now I cry in front of my father, but I don't believe, in spite of people comforting me and thinking I do, that I cry for my father in his coffin. Instead, I am crying for that little boy on the stoop and his father, the one who was not there to protect him, the one who had to work all the time on the docks and who came home tired and grumpy, smelling of gin mills and waterfront rooms where he worked, onions and smelly cheese. He wears a black suit with a white shirt and tie. His pants fall as he speaks, and he must constantly pull up on them. He's got a redness in his face, not from the sun but from drinking and then getting angry. He promises to bring me home a nylon carry-on bag from a Dutch airline when he sometimes works at Idlewild Airport, but he keeps forgetting. But that is not the problem. I need him here. I like to kiss his bristly cheek that, by nightfall, has turned a purple-black from needing another shave. I need him to stand up to my older brothers and the bullies in the neighborhood. I don't need him to play ball, nor do I need him to yell at the other boys. I simply need him here. His presence is needed to let the others know that this is the power behind me. That's the father I mourn.

II.

2

Where the Sky Ends

Early Saturday afternoon on November sixth, in the TWA terminal at Kennedy Airport, I wait for three of my brothers to show. My impatience grows. Where are they? We are flying to Tampa and our flight leaves in half an hour. I look at the front page of *The New York Times,* but I don't have the concentration to read. Dr. Jack Kevorkian (Dr. Death) is arrested by two cops and led away in one photograph. I look at another photograph of the newly elected mayor of New York City shaking hands with a local congressman. I come to page 12, the movie section, and see an ad for *The Remains of the Day* with Emma Thompson and Anthony Hopkins, a movie I had seen a few days earlier. Hopkins plays a dutiful butler named James Stevens. Somehow everything, maybe because I am at the airport where he used to work, reminds me of my father.

My father's name was James Stephens and his father's relatives were from County Clare, but his mother's family were Hopkinses from Mayo. Many in the Hopkins family, who migrated to Ireland from Wales, were named Anthony. The Chief, my father, was not a manservant but a civil servant, yet I am sure that he would not disagree with Hopkins's character James Stevens when the butler says that a man can't consider himself fully content until he has done all he can to be of service to his employer. The U.S.

Treasury got its money's worth when they hired this work-horse of a man.

Now I look at my watch to conjure my brothers faster. I hear myself saying, as if I am my father, "They'll be late for their own funerals." I often like to think—though I may be kidding myself—that we are new and improved versions of our parents.

I am almost never late for anything. I show up too early. Hadn't I arrived at the TWA terminal more than an hour and a half earlier? People in my family are never on time. That thought just proves to me how different we are from each other and why, as adults, my family and I drifted apart.

I may be annoyed that three of my eight living siblings are late for a flight from New York to Florida, but I am not surprised. Chaos is a primary means of expression in this family. Part of that family legacy is to be confused, to stand in a public world like an airport terminal, feeling helpless and alone. Aren't big families the loneliest communities on earth? The idea of smoking a cigarette, even though I have been off them for several years, enters my mind. Another thought pops like one more misfiring brain cell shorting out in my skull: to find a bookie and place a bet. Worse still, I even think of drinking, of having a tall one, something to wash away the pain, to annihilate any feelings.

I already purchased my ticket, brought only a small bag that I will take on the flight with me, and so I look around the terminal for them. As I do this—the airport is not too crowded—I see my brother Joe, and then Brendan, and, lagging behind, brother Tom.

"Where have you been?" I ask.

"Traffic," Joe says.

"Tommy," Brendan says.

"Hey, quit it," Tom says.

Then each of them begins to speak to me all at once, so that I cannot differentiate their voices.

"Let's get checked in," I say. Then I remind them, "Our plane leaves shortly."

That's when it starts.

Brendan says to Tom, "Pick up your bag and let's go."

"I'll pick up my bag when I'm good and ready to pick it up," he answers back.

This is odd only to people who are not our siblings, for Brendan is the youngest, while Tom is the third youngest, and you would think that Tom might boss Brendan.

Tom depends on Brendan for food and shelter because Brendan is the last of the family left on Long Island where Tom still lives. The youngest in the family has become a surrogate father to his older brother, the homeless, the even hopeless, Tommy.

I cannot get over how similar my brothers look: bald, well-built though trim, small but compact, with hawk noses (an Irish beak that people mistake for Mediterranean), their mother's family's small mouth and slight chin. As all the brothers have grown older, we almost seem like sextuplets. (The four of us do not represent even half the children in this big old clan.)

Though I spent my entire life being told that I look just like my father, in fact, I look like these brothers. I am not particularly short or thin—I'm six feet tall and weigh 220 pounds—but everything else is the same: the type of build, the hair loss, the shape of nose and eyes. All of us look more and more, with age, like our mother's kin, the Drews: round, bald, and small.

How odd that time takes us away from our father, even in regard to physical appearance. No one any longer has that Irish peasant face that my father and his father had. What his children do have, though, if not his personality, is his attitude. I cannot believe how much all of us sound like the Chief, how our intonations and even what we speak about is influenced almost exclusively by him—so much so that if I close my eyes and listen to my brothers, it is almost like being in the presence of my father once again.

My brothers gather their bags and shlep over to the check-in counter.

"Move your ass," Joe says to a dreamy Tom, "before the alligators bite it off."

Tom is dreamy from detoxing off of alcohol, though maybe *dreamy* is not the right word for his drifting. Perhaps he really is more stubbornly out of it. I see how scared and disoriented he really is, underneath all of it. His fear reminds me once again—maybe because Tom and I are the dark ones in the family—of that scared little boy I was at the old airport here, when Kennedy was called Idlewild. I thought the airport was where the sky ended. When I was a kid, I rode in a big, old, four-door black Buick on the outskirts of Idlewild Airport. When I reached my hand out the window beyond the swamp cattails, I thought that I could touch the sky. But I am also reminded how fearful I was in the backseat of the car. Are they going to leave me?

Am I their child? Who is my real family? Am I going to burn in Hell for my sins?

We did not own a radio or television at home or have our own car, so I had to ride in a relative's Buick to hear a show. The program was *The Green Hornet,* probably a repeat of an older program. The Green Hornet, his aide Kato, and their rolling arsenal, the Black Beauty, faced another challenge. I am not sure if it was the music or words or simply the ominous air, but the program terrified me, and I started to cry.

I cried like a baby, but I was a baby if a five-year-old child can be considered a baby, so it was all right to cry like that. Now I am a grown-up. Grown-ups don't cry like that. And I will not cry. Even if I wanted to cry, I forgot how to do it a long time ago. Not that I am incapable of crying. In recent years, I have cried while driving alone in my car, in the back rows of dark movie houses where it was safe, even at meetings I attended for my alcoholism. In fact, getting sober had released the controls on my tear ducts. Still, no tears came forth as I waited at the airport for my three brothers.

Where did the fear go?

"So how are you, M.G.?" asks my old buddy Joe.

"I'm okay," I say, but I must be in great denial to say that because I am not anywhere close to being all right.

"I was listening to a John Lennon song," Tom declares to no one in particular. Then he looks at me, as if seeing me for the first time. "You know who John Lennon is, right?"

I do not answer him. After all, he is my younger brother, and I know all about his shtick. I know that he cannot stop talking, for whatever reason, and that before we get to Florida, I will become annoyed with him. But that is projecting, and I am not equipped to project about anything. I am here right now; this is where I live and breathe. I am alive in this moment with my three brothers. I cannot start to think what Tom or Brendan or Joe *will* do. I need to focus on what is happening right now. So I decide not to take the bait from Tom, not to get upset too early with him.

"Take it easy," I say. "Easy does it."

"Easy does it" calms him for a few seconds.

Tom stands there, defenseless, agitated, scared, without an ounce of faith that anything is going to work out all right, that we will get checked in on time (barely), get to our flight, and take off safely, or that we will land, get to our motel room, and eventually meet up with the rest of the family. My two other brothers took him out of a rehab in Hempstead, Long Island, just a few hours ago.

"Hey!" Tom yells. "That guy cut ahead of us."

"I was here long before you arrived," a foreign-speaking man says.

"That's okay," I say to the man. "Tom made a mistake. Of course, you were on line before us."

"Where's that guy from, Mike?" Tom asks. "Where's he going? Is he from India? How come he's not wearing a turban? I thought all Indians wear turbans. Is he going to India? Doesn't he look like the guy who owns a dry cleaners in Hempstead? Hey, where's he going?"

"I don't know," I say, and under my breath, "I don't care."

"What?" Tom asks.

"It's okay," I lie. "Everything's going to be all right."

Brendan, the youngest of all the sibs, tells me—as we wait to finalize our check-in—how they stopped for lunch and how that is why they are late. At an airport diner, Tommy, full of his logorrhea, began to speak to some truck drivers, telling them that the three brothers were about to meet a fourth brother—"and there are a couple of other brothers already in Florida and a bunch of sisters down there too"—in order to catch a flight. Did any of them know his father who had worked for many years at the airport? Of course, the truckers knew whom Tommy referred to because our father was a garrulous, boozy man who talked with everyone.

When my father retired from his airport job, Brendan was the last one in the family left working there. He drove a truck for a shipping company. The other members of the family had drifted away.

This was my father's world, and I can't leave from or arrive at Kennedy Airport without thinking of the little, angry man he once was. I see his impatient, anxious, furious gaze, and I shudder.

But more than thinking of our father, I eye my other connections: these brothers. Joe, the oldest of the three, is a good painter, but in recent years, he has stopped painting and has become a furniture salesman on Long Island, supplementing his income by selling antiques at a flea market in Chelsea every Sunday. Brendan, the youngest, used to drive a truck out of the airport, but now he is in charge of the truckers and has been at his job since he graduated from high school.

Joe had moved recently from Long Island to a town between Albany and the northern Catskills. He is married and has two children; those years when he lived on a hippie farm in rural northeast Connecticut are all but wiped out. He no longer has the flowing, curly mane of dirty blond hair, the Jesus beard, the aroma of weed and brew everywhere. Brendan also has two children, but he is divorced and only sees his daughters on alternate weekends, and his wife has remarried. Tom is too busy staying alive to bother with a relationship. He meets barflies like himself, and because he had once been good looking, he still has little trouble scoring, even moving in with these ladies until even they have had enough of him and ask him to leave. Me, I'm the seanachie, the Keltic scribe.

We wait for our flight to be posted. It turns out that our flight is not leaving from the TWA domestic terminal but rather its international one. We have to go next door. Scrambling to get there, my brothers move about free of luggage because they checked it. I have to lug a heavy bag that grows heavier by the minute as I drag it from one terminal to the next. But this is my own fault. I don't like to check baggage because I can get off the plane and out of the airport faster. We run down a long corridor, right to the end of the spoke from which we will board our jet.

The jet taxis to the runway, only to wait interminably for the okay to take off. Anytime I have to wait on the tarmac, my thoughts invariably dwell on life and death. *Am I ready to go if this is it?* I ask myself. Then I think of all the worldly euphemisms for dying—for death. People used to "pass away." But somehow that innocuous—and meaningless—phrase has been replaced. It is euphemized further. Now I notice that the word *away* possesses its deadly connotations. People simply pass.

Finally, we get a signal to take off, and instantly the jet is airborne.

Brendan and I sit near the middle exit door, Joe and Tommy behind us, with Tommy talking to everyone, telling them where he is going, what he is doing, to attendants and passengers alike. It is fascinating—until it becomes exhausting—to listen to him spray out the non-stop words. I know he can't hear a word anyone says back; he is like an all-night radio-show host, spieling into the night, Benzedrined and full of marijuana, only Tommy is supposedly detoxed and being rehabilitated. Now he tells a flight attendant that I am a writer; he lists some of my titles. All the books he mentions were early works; I know he has almost no knowledge of my recent work.

Listening to Tom, I begin to suspect that there is something seriously wrong with him, not just alcohol, but behind the alcohol. This poor kid has been mangled worse than any of us. Of course, I am not unique in this estimate. Other brothers and sisters over the years have mentioned to me that they thought he has some kind of mental disorder or learning disability. It's incredible that no teacher ever noted this and no one in my family ever attempted to get him help. On his first flight in an airplane, Tom looks pale, nervous, and tense.

Brendan, Joe, and I talk for a while, but soon enough I drift off. I close my eyes; I am not tired and even if I am, I can't sleep. The plane ride is not rough or smooth, just bumpy, just rumbling enough to keep me tense. This is the off-season in Florida, and so, even though it is a weekend at the beginning of November, the plane is not very crowded. Behind me I listen to Tommy talk incessantly with the flight attendants, revealing every intimate detail of his life. Every once in a while I hear Joe tell Tommy that he shouldn't be telling a stranger that. But I'm not awake enough to determine what *that* is, though, knowing Tom, I suspect what he might have said. He probably told the women in flight outfits about being in a detox and a rehab and about everyone's alcoholism and drug addiction, about the crazy family, about living out on the street, about why we were going to Florida. He probably told them, too, that he was *persona non grata* in his family, that he had sponged off all of them so long, he basically had no one left to mooch off of.

"Have you ever heard of the Rolling Stones?" I hear Tom ask a flight attendant.

"Have you ever heard of silence?" she asks.

I open my eyes to see her moving away from him.

"What did I do?" Tom asks.

"You bother people," Brendan says.

"Bother them?"

"You piss them off," Joe says, but I can tell from the sound of his voice that he is teasing his brother, not informing him of any factual details that he might not already know.

"What did I do?" Tom asks again.

"You were born," Joe says. "How's that for starters?"

"I'm scared," Tom says.

He looks like I imagine I looked when I was a little boy driving through the cattails at Idlewild Airport and a scary drama played on the car radio. The sky ended outside the window, just the way it ends outside this plane's window.

Then I hear Tom say, "My father died."

"When?" a passenger asks innocently enough.

"Today," Tom says.

Then it hits me.

"My father's dead," I hear Tom say, almost plaintively, begging for understanding, as though that fact explains everything about him.

3

Who You Are

I sit in my airline seat trying to relax by reading the newspaper. Then I hear Tommy talking to everyone around him. All he can talk about is his family. That is the only subject he knows. He is a man defined by this family. But the family does not treat him well; they tease him, they take his inventory, they scold him, and they make him the butt of all their jokes. That he cannot stop talking has so much to do with the silent treatment his family has given him all his life. They do not listen to him, whether he is complaining, rejoicing, or begging for help because he is in pain. He pays them back by never stopping his chatter.

"My father died today," he says.

"I'm sorry to hear that," a woman says.

"I'm always thinking about my father," Tom says, "but he didn't like me."

"Oh, don't say that," the woman responds.

"No, really," he says. "Ask any of my brothers."

What this woman passenger does not know is that my brother is telling the truth.

Joe says, as if he were a great philosopher, "I heard that men often die just before their birthdays and that women expire right after theirs."

Tom nods, knowingly, as if Joe just offered him a tremendous bouquet of information that he did not already know.

"Where did you hear that?" I ask Joe.

"What?"

"What you just said."

"I don't know," Joe says. "What did I just say?"

"About men dying before their birthdays and women dying after theirs."

"Everybody knows that," he says, then picks up a magazine and pages through it.

Brendan wants a smoke. Joe reads an art and antiques magazine. Tom returns to looking at his magazine.

I see the flight attendant working his way down the aisle, taking drink orders. A good stiff drink might be in order, I think. Maybe several or even many more than that. Perhaps a planeload. Now you're talking, I think. I'll have a gallon of whiskey and two cases of Rolling Rock beer. When the flight attendant gets to me, asking what kind of drink I want, I have a knee-jerk response. I have to bite my tongue. My craving bursts through me, filling my brain with a desire for alcohol, and I feel the craving in my body, even after all these years away from booze. Mostly though, the disease grabs at my soul, jerking it around like a stuffed toy. The flight attendant has my undivided attention. I order a miniature bottle of whiskey and ask for a can of beer. "No, no," I say. "Make that a . . ." I can't get the words out.

"Make that a ginger ale," I say.

The drink signal has—for the moment—passed.

Then the flight attendant moves on.

Who am I to think I can survive a flight to Clearwater, Florida, just because I'm five years sober? I need to remember why I am here. I'm a drunk. Drunks don't handle life well, especially things like living and dying. But why I am here is because I am James Stephens's son Michael; I am also the brother to these other men and women. (And why do I often forget that I have three sisters besides all these brothers?) I was not one of the tough guys in the family. I was the one who cried easily, almost too easily, though I was also the one who could not stop verbally jousting with my older brothers' friends.

But is that who I am? I was that person, yes. And it played into who I would become. And who were they, my family? My father was a ghetto angel from Brooklyn; then he became a tough guy down the piers in Hell's Kitchen. My two older brothers were alternately referred to as either being tough or crazy or both. Jimmy wanted to be on *American Bandstand* with Dick Clark; Peter wanted to be a shortstop for the Yankees; my sister Kaitlin wanted to be a beautician; Joe wanted to own a model-making craft shop; Rosemary, when she became a teenager, wanted to be George Harrison's girlfriend; Tom said he was going to be a singer and guitarist; Peggy wanted to work in physical fitness; Brendan, like Peter, wanted to play baseball.

When very young and asked what I wanted to be when I grew up, I said, "A bum." People laughed. But I was fascinated with hoboes and winos, derelicts and the homeless. Later, I would say, "A poet." Some people probably thought a bum and a poet were pretty much the same thing.

So why am I here? I am my father's son, my siblings' brother, my mother's boy Michael.

Joe sleeps. Brendan reads but is on the verge of sleeping. Tom rattles on, yakking to anyone who will listen. Even the way he indiscriminately talks with people, telling them intimate details about his and our lives, reminds me of my father.

The old man was not a great communicator with his own family. But on the docks he talked with ease to longshoremen, wise guys, government officials, sea captains, ship crew, and passengers alike. In the neighborhood, he chatted with all the neighbors, at least with the ones he hadn't already fought with and resented and to whom he "gave the silent treatment." He particularly talked indiscriminately with anyone at the local gin mill, the more down-and-out they were the better he enjoyed their company and wanted to share the intimate details of his own life. He would talk into the night about one son's report card, another's prowess on the baseball diamond, his daughter's talents at school, his wife's saintliness. He would talk about these things, that is, as long as you weren't a member of his family.

I might be a great loner, but I also made a living as a journalist, talking to other people. These people usually were strangers, and I got on intimate terms with them immediately, pretending to be their best friend in order to make my story. I have done this with countless people, including Mike Tyson, Rick Pitino, U.S. embassy and State Department officials in Seoul, Korea, and the owner of a barbershop in a rough part of Coney Island. I never saw them again after my pieces were filed. Perhaps that is what so unnerves me; I am not that different from Tom and my father. I may have spent a lifetime defining myself in a way to be different than they were, but finally blood is thicker than art. I am my father's son and Tom's brother, no matter how embarrassed that makes me feel. I know that to be true. The problem I have is accepting that fact.

The flight attendant places my ginger ale and salted nuts on the pull-down tray in front of my seat. I thank her, and for a moment, I am given a respite from these feelings. Yet as soon as the attendant moves down the aisle, I am left with these old emotions again. Not only do I become silent around my family—for that has been my role since I was a small boy—I also become fearful and afraid, a scared little boy full of guilt and shame.

What haunts me most are my fears as they relate to this family. After all, my father died of dementia, and by the end, he had no memory. I suppose that, because I am a writer whose stock and trade is the currency of memory, losing one's memory is the scariest thing in the world. Writers, even the major memorialists, are not immune to memory losses. The great transcendentalist Ralph Waldo Emerson, a model of what a nonfiction writer could be, spent the last days of his life without any memory of his accomplishments. So I guess what haunts me going to Florida is this idea of memory. This is true not only because I am a writer, but because of what happened to my father.

By the end of his life, he had forgotten who his wife and children were, and all he could remember were the vague pleasures he experienced, a lifetime ago, of working down the piers in Hell's Kitchen where he had been a big shot for three and a half decades. I realize that he had been dying a long time, through most of his seventies, one little stroke after another, until he became demented and then was institutionalized. Is that what I have to look forward to? I realize, in this plane flying south, that loss of memory is my own anxiety, not my father's. What did he care about memory in the end? For that matter, what did he care about remembering when he still had a mind to use? There was no one more tight-lipped than my father about his autobiography. He might even have welcomed his loss of memory the way drunks embrace oblivion, as if it were the ultimate mother-love.

Am I my memory? Is my memory who I am? Is it dependent—who I am—upon what I remember? If I remember nothing, am I no longer that person I thought I was? If memory goes, am I just a flea, no longer the human I thought I was and hoped to be? Why is memory so important to my sense of being human? Elephants have great memories. Look how they fondle the bones of their herd's deceased. Even dogs remember. Kick a dog and it remembers you forever. Memory is hardly a criterion for being human. It is a tool that writers use, but one cannot measure humanity by the inclinations of people who spend most of their lives isolated from the world, scribbling in notebooks or burning out their irises staring at laptop screens.

This point is made more striking by the fact that my father is dead in his body now. Before that, he was dead only in his mind. Now his body is gone too. When did he stop being my father—when his brain went or when his body did? Or were the mind and body totally irrelevant to being a human? What remains of his soul? Will it float about to bother us—haunt us—or will it find peace at last? My differences with him aside, I hope that my father finds peace and serenity at last.

My father had lived a good life before the strokes hit him a few years ago. For a man from his generation, he had lived a little longer than average, yet those who knew him thought he might have lived still longer and better if he had stopped drinking when he retired. How did a man who never missed work in his life have a drinking problem? Drinking was the reward of that lifetime's efforts. A drinking problem is what his six sons, his three daughters, and his one lifelong wife had; not this U.S. customs inspector who had lived to partake of a fat retirement fund and who even, for the first time in his life, lived the life of Riley.

My brother is back at my ear.

"We're from Brooklyn, right?" Tom asks.

"Right," I say.

"But we didn't grow up in Brooklyn," he observes, again, as if I did not know him.

"Well, you didn't grow up in Brooklyn, but I did," I say.

"You did?" he asks. "When?"

"When I was a kid," I say, "and then Kaitlin and I went back to Grandma's house in Bedford-Stuyvesant every summer."

I think of Brooklyn now, that place we came from. My father was very Brooklyn. He had attitude, as they say, even a chip on his shoulder, right to the very end. He was a street urchin from early childhood until old age, even after he retired and lived the good life in Florida. How odd, though, that Florida is where I have to go to mourn this so Brooklyn of men. I say that more for myself than for my father. Obviously, he came to like, even love, Florida. But I will forever have this notion that he and I were joined by that city in the north where we came from. All of these thoughts are saturated by another feeling: I could not shake the drift in me that wanted to connect with my father, while at the same time I spent my adult life not talking to or seeing him or other people in my family.

The flight attendant from whom I nearly ordered a drink comes down the aisle again.

"Fasten your seat belts, please; we are about to experience turbulence."

As he says this, the cabin rocks and bucks, not wildly, yet enough to capture my attention. The color bleaches out of Tom's face as his knees shake. We had been moving around to stretch. I suggest we sit down and buckle up in the empty seats we find in the rear of the plane. The rear seats catch every movement through the turbulence.

Instead of hearing Tom anymore, I block out what he says and think about other information my brothers and sisters provided me in the last twenty-four hours. My father went from two hundred pounds down to eighty-five pounds, a sister told me. Death was quick, a brother said. It's the dying that took so long, another added. The Chief's personality changed after he had surgery a couple of years ago, Peter told me. Probably a stroke. But no one knows for sure. I think my father would have been happier if he lived part of the year in Florida and part in New York instead of staying in Clearwater year-round. But that is just an opinion, not a feeling or a fact.

I try to read *The New York Times*. The Knicks win their opener; the Nets lose theirs. Then I put the paper down.

My father read the *Times* every day of his New York life. When he moved to Florida, he settled for *The Washington Post*. Though I forever see him as a thick-headed street guy from Brooklyn, he did go to Georgetown for a while, and lest I forget, he spoke fluent Italian. When he took his children on outings to the waterfront and to dine on the *Michelangelo*, *Raffaela*, or *Leonardo*—the Italian ocean liners that docked at Pier 90—he spoke Italian to the waiters, the captain, and the rest of the crew. Perhaps it is these details that I find so hard to reconcile with the picture I have of my father. His rough, surly personality was easily understood in context; I have a harder time reconciling the more disparate parts of his disposition.

"You been to Florida before, haven't you, Mike?" Tom asks.

"Two years ago," I say. "For their fiftieth anniversary."

"I don't remember where I was," he says. "Where was I?"

But I don't know where he was. He was not at the celebration. No one could find him. My mother had loaned him the money to buy an airline ticket, but he spent the money drinking and then disappeared when it came time to go down to Florida. Brendan had looked all over Tom's usual haunts on Long Island, but he could not find his wayward brother. Until that moment, Tom had lived in an abandoned school bus near a golf course. Yet the bus and Tom had disappeared. He did not resurface until after the anniversary, and only then when he ran out of funds and needed a place to sleep, shower, and get a meal. Once he got back on his feet, he disappeared again.

After the ten-minute bout of turbulence, the airplane becomes calm. Tom is unusually quiet. The silence allows me to think on what it is we are doing, where we are going, and why we are here. Joe and I might joke around; Brendan and I might have a good time hanging out together. But there is only one reason for this trip. We are going to bury my father. Even if our feelings for him waiver, we still are paying our last respects. Maybe, though, the respect will grow as the trip progresses, as the connections between me and my brothers, and then my father, are made. Yet life itself feels a bit worthless at the moment and I can't fathom what my purpose is. What does paying one's last respects mean?

Tom says, "I was his fifth son."

"I guess you still are," I say, trying to be cute, but it doesn't pay to be too witty with Tom. He looks at me with great confusion in his knitted brow.

"All of us were born in Brooklyn, right?" Tom asks.

"I wasn't born in Brooklyn," I say. "I was born in Washington, D.C."

"I didn't know that," he says. "I thought everyone was born in that hospital in Bedford-Stuyvesant."

"So you are from Brooklyn," I say.

"Is that why you don't have an accent, Mike?"

I suppose he means that I don't have a Brooklyn or Long Island accent. But I do, only it's slighter than everyone else's. Accent or no, though, I am my parents' son, through and through. If I don't have an accent like my parents and my siblings, I have their look. I have their manners. Our attitudes are the same. We hold the same grudges and resentments. We have the same problems with other people. Though poor, none of us are humble. In fact, we are quite arrogant. This arrogance is combined with a grandiose sense of our own worth, though it is unfortunately wedded to low self-esteem too. Everyone I've ever met from Bedford-Stuyvesant or East New York behaves this way. We are not different from them because we moved farther out on Long Island. We simply took our grudges and resentments and personality disorders with us. Finally, we are all drunks. We are wedded to each other by this disease.

We ride along in the back of the airplane together, Tom and I. He looks out the window, a bit calmer now. I have time to think about my father once again. I wish I had connected with him just once in the terminal years of his life, maybe before the strokes, when some kind of rapprochement might have made sense. Now that thought, given my avoidance of everyone and everything in my family, seems ridiculous, even absurd.

Suddenly, the last time I saw my father in New York— when he was still my father and not this shell of a man I saw in Florida at his fiftieth anniversary—seems so important. He stayed at my apartment overnight for the first and only time. My wife took my parents to the Metropolitan Museum. After going to the museum, I purposely steered everyone down Eightieth Street so that we'd go past his old apartment, number 211. All along Broadway he had asked me endless questions about various stores: Which has the best apples? Where does one find good beef? How much is milk? What brand of bread do we buy? Along with the

questions were verbal sheets of his own memory, not so
much of his own boyhood on the Upper West Side—he
seemed to have no memory of that—but his memories
from the docks and how those memories might radiate
northward from Pier 90 and Forty-ninth Street, clear up to
the Eighties, where he had lived as a very small child. As we
stopped in front of the building on Eightieth Street just off
Broadway and my father looked confused, I explained that
this was where he had lived as a child.

He smiled but didn't seem to register what I had said. An
old toothless woman sucked on a can of beer on the stoop.
He went over to the harridan on the stoop and told her, "I
used to live here."

"A lot of people have lived here, mister," she said.

"With my mother and father," he said.

She asked, "So what?"

He kept talking to the drunken woman, telling her about
his job on the docks and where he lived now, but nothing
about that time when his mother was alive and he was a
small boy on this street. Yet the only surviving photograph
from his childhood was taken on this street, not in front of
this tenement, but down the block and across Broadway,
closer to Riverside Drive and the park, where the exteriors
were more elegant, even magnificent, and so could impress
some immigrant relative back home in the district of
Limerick.

That evening he and I left my apartment, ostensibly to
take a walk, and even though he supposedly did not drink
anymore, we adjourned to a local bar where we each belted
back five quick bottles of beer. He probably drank the five

bottles of beer in less than fifteen minutes. During that time, Jimmy, the day bartender in his late eighties, though still husky and vigorous, caught sight of my father and came over to talk with us. This was unusual because Jimmy, once upon a time the heavyweight champion Jack Dempsey's bodyguard, usually did not care for me. So I knew his interest was all with my father. The bartender asked him if he was Little Stevie; my father looked confused.

"You know," the bartender said, "from the docks down Forty-ninth Street."

Normally my father would use such a recognition to spend the rest of the day and evening in this bar, regaling people with tales of the old days. But my father was a changed man because of the strokes. He told the old bartender that he was not Little Stevie.

After fifteen minutes of quickly drinking bottle after bottle of beer, we went home to dinner.

Later, my wife and mother scolded me for taking my father to a bar. Didn't I know that he had been sick and couldn't control his bladder? My mother said that he'd be pissing—no, that was not a word my mother would use; that was a word her sons would say—that he'd be peeing all over the fold-out couch. The next day a few sisters called to scold me too. In those days, I was still drinking and my attitude was, *So what? He's going to die soon; let him have his beers if they make him happy.* Like the old drunken hag on the stoop on Eightieth Street, I said, "So what?"

We are told to put up our seats, fold up our trays, fasten our seat belts. We are about to land in the Tampa airport.

Tom panics briefly.

"What are we doing?" he asks.

"We're landing," I say.

"Already?" he asks, his voice filled with fear.

After all, he had only gotten into the air and become used to that. Now we are asking him to land.

"It's all right," I tell him. "Just put on your seat belt and everything will be all right."

"Okay," he says, gloomily. Then, to a stranger across the aisle, "That's my brother Mike."

"Oh," the person says.

"He lives in New York," Tom says.

"You don't say," the passenger says, smiling.

"He's . . ."

"Tom, Tom," I say.

"Yeah, Mike?"

"Relax," I tell him.

"Okay," he says, like a child.

When the plane lands, we get off. Tom speaks with another passenger he befriended earlier. She looks like a businessperson and wears a dark suit with a silk blouse.

"Maybe I'll see you at a meeting, Tom," she says.

Tom waves to her. She walks off.

"She asked me if I was here for a vacation or business," he says, laughing.

"What did you say?"

"I told her that we came down for the funeral," he says then runs ahead to catch up with Joe and Brendan.

As I trot down the terminal lobby after my brothers, I

recall another image of my father. Unfortunately, it was long after he stopped being the man I recognized as my father and became an impersonation of the man. It was at the anniversary party, my only other time in Florida and the last time I saw my father alive. It was the last encounter and exchange of words I ever had with him. Our conversation was strange and blank; he didn't know who I was and got angry when I told him who I was. He was thinner, his large head and nose more pronounced, making him appear more immigrant, like someone foreign to his own native land. Even more than the physical change was the mental one. My father had been a tense, explosive, energized creature, unpredictable and verbally prolix. He would be a fighter, I used to think, until the end, but this other man was blankly serene, imploded, the energy in him spent, as predictable as a Gospel on Sunday, but nonverbal and benign. In other words, this was not my father but a man who vaguely resembled my father. In that sense, my father had died quite a few years before this man named James Stephens died, November sixth, in the early morning of Clearwater, Florida.

I said, "I'm Michael, your third son."

He looked as if he might slug me in the nose. He was angry once again, which at least was a familiar quality to witness.

My father did not have a clue about who I was.

"I know who you are," he says.

4

O Florida

Now I am back in Florida.

We land, get our bearings, rent a van, drive to Clearwater Beach, take rooms at an inexpensive motel on the water, with off-season rates still available. Wind runs down the main street at the beach; the sky remains overcast. The strip is empty. At night, after checking into our rooms, we walk around looking for food. It is chilly, and nothing appears open. Finally, we settle for pizza—not very good pizza.

"Florida pizza," Joe calls it.

"The worst," Brendan says.

Try to please a New Yorker with pizza away from home. *Go ahead,* I think.

Tom eats ravenously, not listening to these heresies about the food.

Some of the brothers think of playing miniature golf. But another faction decides to forgo the pleasure. After all, we came to Florida for a funeral, not a five-day holiday. Besides, I am tired, and so is Brendan, and finally Joe admits he is too. We all go to sleep. At least Brendan and I go to sleep. Who knows what Joe had to do with Tommy? Perhaps Joe lets Tom ramble throughout the night, figuring it will exhaust him.

In the morning, it is still cool outside. The sky is gray and overcast. It feels like the weather I just left behind in New

York. I look for a store to buy a newspaper, but I am not having any luck. Finally, I find a drugstore that sells papers. All the newspapers are local. There is no *New York Times,* but I do find a *Washington Post.* Sometimes I forget that Washington is a southern city.

I read the paper as the three northern brothers talk and drink coffee and prepare to face the day. We decide to drive into Clearwater, not to my mother's apartment but to the church where she goes every Sunday. We drive back over the causeway from Clearwater Beach into Clearwater, parking near Saint Cecilia's, right across from the funeral parlor. We walk to the church in the Florida sunshine, the street still empty of people, maybe because all of them are inside the church at this hour.

Joe and Tom walk to the middle of the church where my mother, brother Peter, and sister Rosemary, with her husband, Paul, all kneel in prayer. The two brothers genuflect, enter the pew, kneel, and pray. Brendan and I stay back, hanging in the rear pew. Churches still make me edgy, even though I consider myself a spiritual person. Maybe I should say that because I am a spiritual person, churches make me uncomfortable.

I once heard someone at a meeting say that religion is for people who are scared of going to Hell. A spiritual fellowship such as AA, however, is for people who have already been to Hell. But I do pray. Like my mother and her mother, I have finally learned that prayer is powerful. I pray for the repose of the soul, for suffering to cease, for peace. *Even my father needs peace,* I reason. Perhaps he needs peace more than anyone. After all, he was a man who had no serenity in his life.

Then I bless myself, trying to genuflect as I leave the pew, but because I have not knelt in so many years, my knees will not bend. Perhaps the truth is that my mind does not bend.

I once heard someone say, "I was so low down that kneeling was a step up for me."

I go outside and wait for the others to come out after the Mass finishes.

Coming out of church is the perfect way to see my mother. She is that kind of woman. Yet I don't think she is as typical as people might think. Though she came from a lace-curtain family in Brooklyn—and her family's origin went back deep into Brooklyn—my mother was the black sheep in her tribe. Why, I am not sure, though you could pick it up in subtle ways when you hung around her sisters and brothers. My mother's family treated her differently than they did her siblings. I think that maybe she represented the rebel faction of her gentrified family. Her oldest sister married a *New York Times* executive. Rosie, my mother, the rebel, married my father.

Rebel or not, though, my mother's exterior had all the earmarks of a storybook Catholic girl. When she was young, she was very good looking. There is a photograph on my mantelpiece back in New York that bears this out; in it, she possesses the delicate features of a beautiful colleen. More than that, it attests to a woman with an optimistic gaze, more loving than defiant, though her face is not a passive one. Sixteen pregnancies, nine children raised in Brooklyn and Long Island, and fifty-plus years of marriage to a difficult man had etched themselves on her face. Yet, even with age, my mother still displayed glimpses of that optimistic, Irish Catholic young girl from Brooklyn and a lifetime ago. Small, even tiny—she hovers around five feet tall—she has become very wide, just like her own mother in later years, though this girth does not seem to affect her health.

After coffee and donuts, the family goes back to my mother's place, where we all fall back into the lazy patterns of our childhood. All talk at once, and true to form, I fall silent. I am silent around my family because that was my role in this household, though outside of the family, I am a talker. I am guilty of the same incessant chatter, though mine always comes out when I am not around the family. Here I listen; here I nod my head and convey a sense that I understand. But it is not the social patterns that catch my attention at my mother's condominium. It is that, in this typical Florida complex, my parents had taken their northern world intact into retirement. The condo, minus the endless children from our childhood home, is an exact replica of the house on Long Island. There are the same easy chairs and couch in the living room, the same table in the dining room, and the same La-Z-Boy chair in front of the television set. The same paintings and reproductions hang on the walls, though the photographs have expanded considerably because, now, besides her nine children, my mother has photographs of her many grandchildren, thirteen now that Jimmy has gotten married at age fifty— "Hey, the Irish marry late," he says—and his son Drew runs around the apartment.

To add to the childhood impression of visiting my mother's home, she brings out the kind of food all of us grew up on: white bread, cold cuts, peanut butter and jelly, donuts, coffee—there will be lots of coffee everywhere we go in Florida—coffee cake, and, for the health-minded (this is a dig at me by one of the siblings), a bowl of apples and bananas and oranges. I eat a banana and two apples, drink cranberry juice, and turn down another cup of coffee.

If my mother is a kind of Buddha who stands unperturbed by life's adversities—she calls them "crosses that everyone has to bear"—her children are more like their father. They possess enormous energy that sometimes translates into agitation. I often thought that self-righteous anger, for instance, was a family trait before I learned that it was an aspect of alcoholism. I also thought that a hair-trigger rage was an ethnic characteristic until I heard about post-traumatic stress disorder, something that does not happen to combat soldiers only. I'd be willing to bet that anyone who comes from a big family, whether it be mine or a more privileged one like Robert and Ethel Kennedy's family, has a certain amount of combat stress. But other than my mother, there are no Buddhas in residence in this pod. All I have to do is look around the room to see the effects of our upbringing. Even greetings have an edge. I look around my mother's condo to see if I am right about this. Attitude resides everywhere.

My second-oldest brother, Peter, sits in the La-Z-Boy chair in front of the television while Joe sits on one of the couches. Tommy and Brendan are at the dining-room table with Rosemary and her husband and their two large grey-hounds. On the couch, next to me, sits my mother's cousin Eddie.

Of course, I never called this man Eddie in my life. He was addressed as Father Eddie. (Like my uncle Andy, my mother's youngest brother, he is a Franciscan priest, my mother's family being big on Franciscans.) But no matter how I address him, I cannot say that I know him well. I saw him only a few times in my childhood. I thought that he was Grandpa Drew's cousin, but really he was my mother's first cousin.

He is in his eighties, retired, and living down here now; years ago he had been a professor of German, teaching at Saint Bonaventure College in western New York state, and we speak briefly about Heinrich Heine (he corrects my pronunciation of the surname). I recount for him how I found an essay about the German poet that my great-grandfather Richard McCann, a New York lawyer and journalist, wrote when he was a student at Columbia.

The old priest chats with people in the living room, but my attention is drawn to my brother Peter in the other room. We are the closest in age and, at least when we were young, had hung out together more than any of my other brothers and sisters. Peter's teeth had been pulled recently, and because he is awaiting new ones that are being made for him, he is toothless.

I know, because we all have such bad teeth—"the curse of the Irish," my mother said—that a similar fate awaits me. I suppose I want to see how he looks and how he fares without the teeth. The truth is that I want all my own poor teeth to be pulled and to be done with it.

But Peter looks so thin, grizzly, and tough. Usually garrulous around family members, he is moody and silent because of the teeth situation. Still, I don't expect that he'll brood at the periphery of the conversation for long.

I had enormous grudges against my two older brothers when I was quite young. They often used me as their human punching bag. If I was not getting my ass kicked out on the street daily, then I came home to have one of them torture me in a bedroom. They might twist an arm or bend a wrist, get me into a headlock or a half or full nelson, or give me a pink belly.

By the time we were teenagers, though, we had become friends. I had come to admire my two older brothers. They both had reputations. Jimmy was considered a real tough guy, a dangerous street fighter. Peter was thought of as one of the craziest kids in the neighborhood, a guy who would try anything for a kick or a laugh. Such brothers gave you a high status on the street.

Also, they were my insurance that the bullies no longer could pick on me. If they did, Jimmy or Peter might look them up.

Before he came down to Clearwater, Peter had been driving a cab in New York City and, for the last months of his stay in the city, had lived in a single-room-occupancy hotel on my corner, so I had seen him occasionally. When I first got sober about five years earlier, he had been sober, too, for about a year or two. His history was to go in and out of sobriety. He was the first person in our family to go to Alcoholics Anonymous, but he never bought the program. Something about it never sat right with him. He would put together a few weeks, even several months, and sometimes even a year or two, but never more than that, and then he would be off to the races, out on another run.

I often think his inability to stay clean has to do with his asthma. The medications he has to take often trigger a drink signal, set up the compulsion again. At any rate, who am I to judge Peter or, for that matter, anyone else in this family? We all are in the same drunken boat; we all are members of the same clan. All of us suffer from the same disease.

Peter had colitis in high school and missed two years of school. After I left Chaminade, an elite Catholic prep school in Mineola, to attend Herricks, the public high school in New Hyde Park, I entered the same classrooms as my older brother. He unquestionably became the wildest student in the school. His forte was taking off his clothes— at a party, basketball game, even in a school version of Thornton Wilder's *Our Town.*

Though I had been an excellent student before going to Herricks, at the public high school I was not only a good student but also Peter's brother. This conferred upon me a status with the juvenile delinquents and made problems for me with teachers and administrators. I recall a French teacher, my first week at Herricks, accusing me of cheating because I had scored highly on the first test, and no one else in the class did. How could I have done that? I was Peter's brother, and though Peter was bright, he was the class cutup.

I was relegated to a social status with the hubcap stealers, not the students who excelled academically, even though that is where I had resided for the first nine years of school. I had never been less than the third-highest student at school. Suddenly I found myself bottom-fishing with boys who neglected all academic work and were interested only in shop and auto mechanics.

That was the world Peter and I grew up in. After high school, I went off to college, and he began to work in the city, eventually winding up as a stagehand at the Metropolitan Opera House, where he met his future wife, a dancer, with whom he eventually had four children. They have been divorced for many years, but he still keeps in touch with his children, all of whom seem to adore him.

The last time I saw him we met for breakfast at a luncheonette on Broadway called Key West, and he berated me, after I had bought him his breakfast, for not letting him stay at my apartment and not helping him out. (He had been strung out on crack and other drugs, besides indulging his alcohol jones.) But I was out of work, low on funds, and in recovery myself, and I didn't see his staying with me as a good idea. I had my own family to worry about. Peter told me that I was a much better person when I was a drunk.

"At least you had a heart then," he said; then he stomped off.

In contrast to my brother's cynical take on things—not an atypical response in this family—relatives of my mother's generation invariably produced an optimistic response to their lives. Take that old priest in the living room. Father Eddie tells us a story about his and our mother's childhood, some outing the family made to Coney Island. His story idealizes Brooklyn, turning it into a place that I have never heard of or seen except in my mother's own fairy tales about it. Theirs was a Brooklyn of horse-drawn carriages, street-cars, gaslight, and elegant brownstones that never smelled of mildew and mold like the brownstones of my own child-hood in Brooklyn.

Suddenly Father Eddie stops talking and looks at my brother Joe across the room. The old Franciscan adjusts his glasses as if he can't believe his eyes. He directs his remark at my brother Joe.

"Why, it's Billy Drew!"

Someone corrects him, saying that it is Joe, our brother, not Billy Drew, our cousin. Besides, Joe and Billy do not look that much alike.

"I mean Uncle Billy," Father Eddie says.

There again, I think that he is slightly off, for while my brothers and I now resemble, because of our baldness, our maternal uncles—Uncle Billy being one of them—none of us bears that strong a resemblance to this uncle.

Besides, Uncle Billy, who used to live at our house on Long Island when he was not working on merchant ships going around the world, had been murdered in the Sea of Japan, they said, off the coast of Pusan during the Korean War. Joe does not look like Uncle Billy.

Then I realize that my mother's cousin, this old Franciscan priest whom I have met only a handful of times in my life, does not mean *my* Uncle Billy but *his* Uncle

Billy, his own mother's brother. Though it takes me awhile to get untangled by the ropes of genealogy in these remarks, I come to see what Father Eddie really means—*my* own grandfather William Drew, *his* Uncle Billy.

Only recently I had been given, by one of my cousins, a photograph of this grandfather. The photograph was taken at his wedding around 1913, and other than the old-fashioned high collar and the stiff, formal, vested suit, it could have been my brother Joe dressed in a period costume. I mean, of course, a Joe before he became a hippie and grew wild, stringy, long, dirty blond hair and a scraggly beard. Still, the resemblance was remarkable, even for relatives.

"Yes, yes, yes," Father Eddie said, "he looks just like Uncle Billy."

Peter starts to reminisce about one of the priests at Saint Aidan's, the parish on Long Island to which we had belonged and where all of us had received eight years of parochial education. My brother goes off on a diatribe about this parish priest, and if you didn't know my brother, you might think he was talking about someone with whom he had an encounter yesterday, but since he is nearly fifty years old and the event he describes happened in our childhood, he really is referring to an event that happened nearly forty-five years ago. He believes that the parish priest willfully sold our family two green-and-gold satin school jackets with the school name misspelled; that the priest would not have given, much less sold, these jackets to any other parishioners but us; that he did it to us because we were new in the parish, freshly arrived from our Brooklyn ghetto where we probably didn't know how to spell, and so it wouldn't matter. This is the kind of spin my brother wants to put on the story.

The old Franciscan sits there mildly confused, lost in the shuffle of voices, his hearing not good enough to pick out which one of these relations says what.

As Peter goes on with his diatribe against the parish priest for selling us the two jackets with the misspelled school name, another brother interrupts.

"But who cares?" the brother asks.

"You can't talk to me like that," Peter says. "I'm your older brother." (I have to laugh at this remark because I have heard Tommy say it to Brendan at least three times in the past twenty-four hours; it is a kind of familial refrain.)

My mother flits in and out of the living and dining rooms, unveiling pound and coffee cakes, filling people's coffee cups, bringing ashtrays for the smokers, asking if we need anything else. She smiles. She laughs nervously, that signature laugh of the Drew family, an edgy exclamation at the end of a sentence or phrase. My tiny, sweet, heartbreakingly beautiful mother is getting old and wrinkled, but she never seems to lose her simple, direct tenderness for everyone.

What is remarkable about my mother is not her appearance, though. Her look is really too modest to reveal much of anything about her. Not only is she humble, she is also an exceedingly deferential woman. Yet her most revealing quality is her personality. My mother is an optimist. Nearly everything in life will work itself out and be all right. This was true when we were children and came home with our skulls bashed in, fingers hanging off by nerve endings, broken ribs, ankles, and legs, or had the police chasing after us.

It is still true today. Her demeanor is slow and easy, very gentle and upbeat. When she used to booze, it was often hard to tell when she was drunk because, drunk or sober, she had that same positive outlook, though I'm told that after I left home her drinking put her into despondency. No wonder the southern belles of Clearwater liked her so much; her speech might be Brooklyn, but her slow, easy manner was of the South, gentrified and soothing.

I listen to Peter, watch the old priest, see my mother come in and out of the rooms with cake and coffee, and I wonder why we are here. Our father died the day before. In the morning, we all plan to travel to the funeral parlor across from Saint Cecilia's church to hold a good, old-fashioned Irish wake for the dearly departed. Is it denial or indifference that propels everyone in the room? I think perhaps it is a dollop of both.

As Peter tells his endless story of resentment for a parish priest who sold him a defective green-and-gold pseudo-silky baseball jacket, I remind myself that I, too, have a way of latching on to a resentment and, terrier-like, not letting go. I spent a lifetime resenting my father. Now it is time to pay the piper. It is also time to come to terms with the dead. How does one maintain a resentment toward a dead man? I start to realize, sitting there in my mother's living room, seeing the old Franciscan priest and Peter animatedly talking, that I have to plan for a long five-day siege. The wake starts tomorrow morning.

That's what makes this Florida thing so odd.

"Ask Michael," Peter says, though his remark is not really addressed to anyone in the room.

It is his rhetorical flourish.

"Ask him," he says. "He was there. He grew up in that house. He went to that school. He remembers those damn green-and-gold satin jackets with the misspelled name on them. Tell them, Michael. Tell them about those jackets."

But I do what I always do. I am silent. I also think. Whenever I was quiet as a child, I thought too. My brain reeled with images, words, reflections. I thought about family. Our family was no family in any conventional sense, nor was it a family in any sense of a criminal enterprise. Really what we were was a lose amalgam of people who looked, talked, and behaved like each other. But what, finally, did we have in common? I was not sure; I still am not sure. My father had been the head of our family in a historical sense, but what he had not realized was that he was the father of the family in a mythological sense too. He was a kind of legend, not only in the family and among our relatives, but also in the neighborhoods where we lived. The legend was more Aristophanic than Sophoclean, more buffo than tragedian. I sit listening to Peter rail against a priest from a lifetime ago while another old priest sits there, not in his clerical collar, but in tacky Florida golfing gear, wondering who these people are who call themselves the children of his cousin Rose.

"Tell them, Michael," Peter says.

Once again, I say nothing. I want to speak, but speaking is not a primordial response in me. Michael has to remain silent, a great mystery. Everyone has a role to play in a family, especially a big family, and silence is the part I was given and that I played so well. I did not judge, did not vilify, did not criticize or complain. I was silent. Silence is a good way to greet the enormous void of attending your father's funeral.

Suddenly, though, I recall what Peter said to me in that luncheonette back in New York City a year or so earlier: I was a much better person when I was a drunk; at least I had a heart then. Wasn't that just where my disease, this illness, this alcoholism, wanted me? The disease had me where it wanted me now. In the midst of my family, it says, "Have a drink, Michael. You don't matter anyhow. You're a bum. A louse. A nobody. They're all nobodies, but you are the biggest nobody of all. So let's drink and be merry. For tomorrow will never come."

But tomorrow we would begin to mourn my father.

5

Meditation on the Harp

I suggest to Joe that we go out and do something for the rest of the afternoon. The next day we would be locked in the funeral service all day, and the day after that would be the Mass and then the service at the cemetery. He agrees. He mentions visiting the Salvador Dali Museum in Saint Petersburg, the next town over. This seems right; in fact, it is inspired, even brilliant. You would not look at Rembrandts, thinking about my clan; you would not search out the Impressionists. Picasso and Matisse make no sense in our world. Salvador Dali does.

If I were looking for a movement to characterize my family, I'd choose surrealism. A writer friend once described it as the juxtaposition of two or more objects in a way that they are not ordinarily perceived. I think he meant literary surrealism, but the definition was fine for my blood relations. A fish rains down on a man in a bowler hat dressed like a banker. A clock melts across a tree. A couple who should not have had any children have sixteen of them, and nine live. Surrealism is born.

Take our childhoods. A lawn mower might be found in a closet, a yard rake in the kitchen. That textbook for history, the one you could not find the entire school year, shows up on a pantry shelf. Laundry was found in the garage. Tools for the car were in the refrigerator. A bed might be piled sky-high with clothing. Therefore, you slept in a closet.

I go along this excursion, partly as a joke, partly as an homage; the Chief, I think, and nearly all his children agreed, was an absurd man. It was a quality that he bequeathed to his children whole-cloth, with no strings attached. Each of us, to various degrees, has a weird sense of humor, all of it fueled by the ridiculous.

Joe's sense of the ridiculous seems to be in its glory this afternoon as he regales me with stories about our father, his escapades, his bons mots, his observations, and his sayings. One of the more famous incidents—this one made the local papers and then the evening television news—was when he started up his Dodge Dart, got out of it, and went back inside the house for coffee one morning.

Some of the children said he went back inside to finish his breakfast; others said it was to take a shit. Really, it doesn't matter. When he went back outside, the car popped out of park and went into overdrive gear, and since the wheel was turned a certain way, the car rolled around in circles, chasing after its driver. The Chief ran in the same arc, though slightly ahead of the car. A saner man might have stepped out of the way; a dumber man might have tried to stop the car. Our father chose to run ahead of it as if in some Buster Keaton moment—the machine personalized and anthropomorphized and out to get the Chief for the way he treated it; the car was trying to run him down.

We exit from an interstate highway onto Fourth Street South, turn right at a light, and go six blocks to Eleventh

Avenue South, and at Great Explorations, "the Hands On Museum," we turn left. It is downtown, the waterfront of Saint Pete. We come to the Dali museum.

My brother parks the car in the lot and we go inside a large, modern room; all of the walls are covered with Dali paintings.

Joe is not painting now, but he used to be quite a good painter, and I suspect, if he got back to it, he still would be. My younger brother sells furniture at flea markets in New York City. I'm close to Joe in age, and though we had not done much together as kids, we did become good friends once he moved into the city after high school to attend the School of Visual Arts. It was during this period—I lived in an abandoned building on lower Second Avenue—that Joe lived in his own abandoned building on the western edge of Canal Street. Only Joe was far more ingenious than I was; all I had managed to finagle was a set of keys that admitted me into my abandoned building. Joe had commandeered his building, borrowing water from one adjacent building, electricity from another. Despite his being a degenerate hippie reeking of herb and zonked on acid, the more working-class elements of the family were drawn to Joe's crash pad too. Thus on any night one might visit him and find the drunken Chief himself holding court on a flea-bitten couch in the living room when he was transferred from Hell's Kitchen to the piers in Greenwich Village, years before he was exiled to work at Kennedy Airport. To encounter my father in this decrepit location was like meeting Hamm from Samuel Beckett's *Endgame*. Forget about the Pope of Greenwich Village. He was the Emperor of the Waterfront.

A gaping hole in the second floor looked directly down upon the first floor, an empty storefront that Joe used for a painting studio. If my father was not there, you might find our older brother Peter camped out, hiding from the law. The old man's excuse was that he was working the piers below Morton Street, and this was a convenient place to crash instead of taking the train all the way out to Long Island.

This wonderful crash pad reminded me of Gulley Jimson in *The Horse's Mouth,* though others found it to be like an urban version of Ken Kesey's funny farm in Oregon. Drugs oozed out of every crack in the bare walls; rats and vermin skittered across the rafters. The deafening traffic outside on Canal Street inched its way toward the Holland Tunnel, though usually everyone was too trashed on drugs and booze to notice. Once, visiting Joe on the West Side, he invited me to dinner; he lowered himself through a skylight into the luncheonette next door, the same place from which he boosted his electricity, and came back with ham, eggs, Cokes, lettuce, and tomatoes. Amazingly, the owner never caught on, even when Joe and his friends descended through the skylight, partying all night long, making ice-cream sodas, grilling hamburgers, concocting BLTs from Heaven above.

But it didn't stop there. After Joe got busted and sent on probation out of the city—the judge told him that he wanted to remove him from the pernicious world of Art that had corrupted his good Catholic mind—he wound up spending the next twelve years on an equally déclassé, though always wonderful and unpredictable, crash farm in rural northeastern Connecticut. The land was complete with a hippie garden, an old workhorse he rode bareback (the horse) and naked (my brother), and an endless pack of dogs he owned from Scotties to Russian wolfhounds that were forever being gunned down by the local farmers and the Ku-Kluxers, who unfortunately had a toehold in that part of Connecticut. But eventually the party ended; the piper needed to get paid, and Joe wound up leaving the farm and coming back to Long Island, first to get sober, then to find work, and finally to settle down with his family. He is married, has two children, and lives in upstate New York, but he comes down to the city once a week to sell his antiques.

I remember that, when he painted, Joe's sense of color was sublime, very delicate and light. The colors were pastel and feminine, even "beautiful." These are not, normally, concepts I associate with the life of my brothers, who tend to be rougher at the edges and tougher, more hardened at the core. That is probably why I get along with Joe so well. We are the creative types in the family, though it might be said that each one of my brothers and sisters has some kind of artistic streak. Some play music; others dance. I write; Joe painted. I often think that our oldest brother, Jimmy, might have made a good actor with his deep, booming voice and his huge, operatic body. Peter seems to have some kind of penchant for the stage too. The girls are, like Joe, more visually oriented. Tom played a guitar. I know that Brendan was a jock, mostly baseball, but I'm sure he has some kind of creative urges. Like Joe, he was into beautiful objects, in Brendan's case, blue glass bottles.

But of all my siblings, Joe is the one I am most comfortable around. His sense of humor is dark and bizarre. He likes to be irreverent. As we walk from one surreal painting to the next, he comments. At a painting entitled *Portrait of My Sister,* he says, "It kind of looks like Kaitlin," our own sister. *The Disintegration of the Persistence of Memory,* with its melting clocks, oyster-colored nonhuman figures, fish, and rhino horns, reminds him of our childhood home where the juxtaposition of objects was, as I have said, surreal.

Joe takes the extravagant imagery of Dali's paintings and applies them to our personal lives.

Did I remember the time our mother left a plastic dish on the hot stove and it melted? The plate flopped over the porcelain top of the stove.

"It was like a Dali," Joe says.

I laugh, though I do not recall this event. Perhaps it never happened. Joe was merely storytelling, spinning out a tale. The point is, it could, should, might have happened. Anything was possible in that household, that fallen domain we grew up in on Long Island. Is that why Dali's paintings look so realistic to us?

When I laugh at Joe's comments, I realize that why I'm there is really far from my mind. Being in Florida lends an unreality to everything. This could not be explained away by the fact that I am more familiar with oaks and elms and robins and bluejays than palm trees and pelicans and herons. The orange is one of my favorite fruits. I prefer the blue-green water of the Gulf to the dark gray-green color of the North Atlantic Ocean.

But I also realize that when people first die, nothing but unreality surrounds the circumstances, particularly the lives of the survivors. There really is no adequate vocabulary to explain what happens. No amount of education prepares one for the ontological moment. That I did not get along with this parent does not matter. In fact, it makes the situation worse. I must feel bad for someone I did not particularly like. I must mourn for the dead in the way that others do for their loved ones. And I am not talking about a friend or acquaintance. I am referring to my own father. He is the corpse that none of us has dealt with yet. One moment you are alive, if not well, and the next you are gone, the life force flown out of you, dead, as they say, as a doornail. Kaput!

I find myself becoming quiet. Joe goes off in one direction, and I walk the other way. The main room in the museum is quite large, with paintings all around it. I see him on the other side of this large room, admiring the smaller paintings like *Morphological Echo* and *Paranonia,* works I admired moments earlier. I stand in front of a four-teen-foot-high painting entitled *The Discovery of America by Christopher Columbus,* overwhelmed by its sheer volume as it towers over me. It is a kind of homage to Velázquez, Columbus the possible Catalonian (not the Italian), and even pop art. Though I have never been a great fan of Dali's, I admire this painting the same way I admired the smaller, more intimate paintings across the room.

Nearly all his titles affect me. One painting is called *Autumn Sonata,* and it renders, in the quintessential dream-like landscape of a surreal painting, a basilica, an arch, crip-ples, men fighting on horseback, boats, low-slung mountains, all of it meticulous and slightly larger than a postcard. But since I am a writer, not a painter, I think of words, not images. I am not thinking about my father. Perhaps I am too consciously not thinking about him. I focus on that word *surrealism*. How often it is misused to describe more journalistic events. Something "weird" is called "surreal," when, looking at these paintings by Dali, it is plain to see that the surreal is not weird so much as dreamy. In that sense, the dead become surreal, not weird but dreamy. All that remains of them are the shadows they cast inside of us, just like the ominous shadows cast across the theatrical boards of some of these paintings and their landscapes. A dead father is like a melting clock.

Puzzle of Autumn contains a Turneresque sky gone a jaundiced yellow. But the one that really catches my attention is entitled *Meditation on the Harp*. A man and woman pose, the woman naked. In front of them stands a deformed, cone-headed figure with big feet. The painting instantly brings to mind some dark relationship I have with my own parents, the attractions and repulsions, the shame and guilt. Also, I cannot help but think of how the term *harp* is often used as a derogatory name for the Irish and that my father was nothing if he was not a harp.

Being left alone, surrounded by strangers and these oddly beautiful paintings, I reflect upon the past twenty-four hours. It might be more accurate to say that the last twenty-four hours grab and shake me awake. I have not spent any extended time, other than holiday visits, with anyone in my family since I was fifteen years old. No one in my immediate family had died before my father. My only experiences with the death of relatives, even in middle age, were to attend the funerals of my grandfather when I was boy, a stepgrandmother in my adolescence, and more than ten years earlier, my maternal grandmother. My other relatives did not so much die as move to the suburbs, never to be heard from again.

That morning, after I had come back from looking around for newspapers to read, Joe and I went out for an all-you-can-eat breakfast at another hotel before heading off to see my mother and other family members at the Sunday Mass. That breakfast place, it turned out, was significant. It literally was the last place I had ever seen my father alive, at least the last place where I saw the man with my father's name. (My real father was last seen that day I took him drinking in my neighborhood bar in New York City.) I had come down to Florida for the first time, even though my parents and most of my siblings had been living there for years. I am a bit of a prodigal son, I guess, although no one was going to lose sleep over whether I attended their family gatherings or not.

The family book on me goes like this: Michael is considered odd, even in this very odd family. He writes books, lives a separate life from their lives. In essence, he betrayed the working-class covenant by presuming to be something other than what the family had thought he would become: perhaps a cop, a fireman, or, more likely, a high-school English teacher after he graduated from the state teachers' college. His becoming a writer does not make him any different, though. After all, this is a truly outcast bunch, none of them fitting into the mainstream.

73

We sat eating breakfast, looking at the Gulf outside the windows. Pelicans and herons dove for fish. The sky remained overcast and gray. No sun shone. It was as cold outside as it had been in New York City the day before. I watched as a pelican climbed ponderously skyward, paused in the air, then dove, bulletlike, into the water below, catching a fish in its oversized bill.

The room was a bright pastel and it had an airy, high-ceilinged quality to it. The customers were the everyday variety of working-class and middle-class tourists and retirees, not an exotic face among them. Off-season drew only those like ourselves, because of family obligations.

Herons stood on the beach outside as still as lawn ornaments. Occasionally, one might shift a leg; otherwise they did not move at all. I could not think of a more foreign landscape. I could not help thinking about that last time I was here in this room for their fiftieth anniversary, and I watched my father eating absentmindedly.

My father smiled, sitting at his table. His smile was vacant, not tossed at anyone. He did not talk. Speech had escaped this grand old shmoozer. He appeared benevolent, even kind. Certainly he was calm, none of his jittery animation existed anymore. If someone entered the room without knowing who he was, one might find him a nice-looking, cheerful old coot, a bit dotty, but otherwise quite okay.

Though my father did not speak, my mother filled in the blank spaces for us.

"He may have lost his memory," she said, "but he never lost his appetite."

My mother said these words as though they were positive signs. Memory was not important, but an appetite was. Memory was a burden, but an appetite that could be fulfilled was the culmination of these Depression-era dreamers. They had not starved, after all. They had survived the Depression and the World War, the fifties, the sixties, clear up to the nineties.

As my mother spoke, my father ate oatmeal, slurping and happily making noises. He dunked his toast into the coffee, something he would have smacked us for when we were children. Though our household was chaotic and seemed to have no rules, my father could be unusually strict with us at times. These times were when he was not drinking. Once he was drinking, he might become violent, hitting us liberally, but all rules flew to the wind. When he was not drinking, the rules came back.

My father poured ketchup on his eggs and stacked piles of bacon and sausage on the side of his plate as if they were monuments to his hunger. The strokes had taken away his memory, his biography, and the past, but hunger was a lower-brain function, a product of the brain stem.

Maybe the old man eventually came to an understanding with Florida, but I could not relinquish the thought that what bound us together was that we were both New Yorkers. We loved Manhattan, a borough to which others in the family were either indifferent or hostile. Sometimes I forget and think that my family members are New Yorkers too. But they are not. They are Long Islanders. Their accents are similar and, occasionally, the attitudes coincide. But New York is a city—The City. Long Island remains the essence of the

American suburb, a place where you depend on a car to get around. Suburbanites adore material objects. The grittier spiritual life of a city belies this love of tchotchkes and cars. This might simply mean that life often is cheap in the city; your good looks, your money, your fame mean nothing to a street kid out to cut or shoot you. Sick as it may sound, I like that kind of edge that the city provides. But Florida is more like Long Island than New York City, and perhaps that is what baffles me most about my father's ultimately coming to terms with it. There was no one more New York than the old man, and no one knew the city as well as he did, not even I who have lived my entire adult life there.

Perhaps that is why I am at the Salvador Dali Museum with my brother Joe. I cannot handle—because I cannot fathom—Florida. Coming to this museum is a compromise. It is not New York City—people in Manhattan might scoff at Dali's paintings—but it is not quite Florida either. I suppose I am still thinking of my literary friend's definition of surrealism. I am willing to settle for an odd juxtaposition in order to get by in Florida. I cannot accept the thing itself, but I am willing to ride along with it if I have these paintings to buffer the experience of Florida. Yet probably Florida has nothing to do with it. The paintings act as a buffer between me and death.

If my father did not die with great dignity, then he died fighting all the way. That is something, I guess, fighting being preferable to surrender. When you surrender, you are gone. He gave the good fight, they said. He went out like a trooper. Of course, none of this is true. He did not give a good fight nor go out like a trooper. From what I heard, he died empty-headed, not even knowing if he was alive or dead. The seam between life and death had been erased for him. He went out in a hazy breath of intoxicated fury, fighting ghosts instead of substances. The substances had done him in.

I stand in front of another huge Dali painting, *The Hallucinogenic Toreador*. Venus de Milo multiplies herself. She looks like the figure on a Venus pencil, but with her shadows, she appears to turn into a bullfighter. Art and mass reproduction are issues of this century, but in my family, reproduction was everything. My mother and father were profligate human beings, throwing themselves into a life of reproduction in a way I have seen nowhere else. I don't know personally of any human being other than my mother who was pregnant sixteen times. Sixteen is the number she tells me. Perhaps it was even higher. And my parents married when they were considered old by their generation, in their late twenties.

I don't think Yeats had my parents in mind when he spoke of the "grand gesture," that most Irish of actions, full of grace and dedicated artfulness. But how do I, their son, explain this productivity to a world unfamiliar with such inclinations? Instead of it being grand, perhaps it was simply an enormous gesture. Maybe like Henry Ford grinding out Model Ts, it only had to do with mass production. If you make enough children, some of them might prosper and take care of you late in life. Yet I think that my father, especially, would rather die than depend on one of his children for help. Finally, like these Dali paintings, my parents simply were extravagant, overblown, yes, surreal.

What are the others doing on this day? I don't know. I imagine that they stayed at my mother's condominium, telling stories to each other for the rest of the day. The stories would be ones everyone was familiar with. They might drink coffee, smoke, eat coffee cake, and talk. My family liked nothing better than talking. Joe and I went to the Dali museum. I do not think that one choice is better than the other. They did what they had to do in order to survive, to endure the terrible weight of a personal death. We did what we had to do.

I discover two things: Dali was not, as I had thought for years, a flimflam artist, but an artist who had a shrewd—even an ingenious—eye for his own time. Andy Warhol and Salvador Dali capture the twentieth century as well as any visual artists I can think of. One sees it as a joke; the other as a preposterous dream. Neither is completely right; more important, neither is completely wrong. The other thing I learn to do is to look at my father without all the venom I had gathered in me for so many years. He was a man, a human being, and he had died.

I often used to hear this old fellow at AA meetings say that alcoholics were like anyone else, only, he said, "We are all more simply human than otherwise."

It was not so much that my father was more simply human than otherwise. I see that all of us are.

As we walk toward the van in the parking lot, Joe and I are joined in our moment before grief. We laugh. I think that laughter is as good as any emotion to come to terms with the fact that all of us are here only for a blink of the eye; then we are gone.

Driving out of Saint Pete, I think of Dali and Warhol, and I decide to include Marcel Duchamp in that visual triumvirate that paid lip service to the century. I am in Florida, deep at the ass end of the millennium, waiting to become profound and significant in the next great age, but knowing, too, that insignificance and banality are as likely a destination as great discovery. I realize that no one is going to say anything about my father except me. I am his eulogist in this sense, outside the family. If I do not praise him, he will be condemned. What a terrible burden, I think.

As with so many other abused children, one part of me is filled with rage and outrage, the other part a mixture of wonder and love. In many respects, our devotion (my siblings', I mean) is greater than children who truly loved their parents. We were so lost, his parental warmth—basically a chilly wind in winter—was all we had. The Dali paintings remind me of this, too, because each of them, being surreal, is about dreams, and we all know that dreams have only two subjects: sex and death. That's just what family is too: sex and death, procreation and dying, giving birth and burying the dead. Unlike Mediterraneans who would have had the decency to take along a mistress or two, we are puritanical Irish Catholics; we only know how to make babies from sex. Yet who could deny the erotics of this afternoon? Young women browsed those eerie works, commenting in Spanish, Portuguese, French, and English about the bloody imagery on the sometimes oversized canvases, particularly those monstrously heroic ones about Columbus and nuclear war. How do you leave the twentieth century? By coming to

Clearwater to bury your father and then visiting the Dali museum.

On the way back to the motel on the beach, I buy a pair of cross-training sneakers at a factory outlet, I eat McDonald's french fries and some chicken fajitas, I wonder why I have yet to taste a good orange or some fresh-squeezed orange juice, and I wonder why I am feeling nothing about being on the Gulf Coast of Florida, and even less about my father's death.

6

Clearwater Blues

I wake in the Econolodge motel to the sound of men working outside the window. Brendan sleeps in the bed next to
mine, while two other brothers sleep next door. It is just
after sunrise, though it is not bright out. I look out the
window and see a few men struggling with a rusty boiler to
get it on the flatbed of a truck. They curse and shout as if
it were midday, not six in the morning. Brendan grunts,
not awake but clearly disturbed by the noise too. I get up
and go to the bathroom. My sleeping brother, ordinarily a
tough guy, looks so innocent and young, almost like he did
when he was a little kid and I was his big, teenage brother.

More than twelve years separates me from Brendan.
What I learned talking to him the night before, though,
was not about our differences, but how similar we are. I
often thought that his upbringing was less chaotic because
everyone, except Peggy and a few strays, had left home by
the time he became an adolescent. My mother was sober;
my father either controlled his drinking or had briefly
stopped. With that enormous number of children grown
up and gone from the roost, money flowed into the house
for the first time since my parents met in the early 1940s.
The rooms were not so cluttered with bodies and their
accoutrements. Williston Park must have been almost idyllic. But, of course, it was not. None of us seemed to get

enough love from my mother and we received almost no affection from our father. Yes, she loved us, our mother; there is no question about that. But that love was equally divided between ten people. Love was not a concept my father was familiar with at all, I think, because he had grown hard, on the street, on his own, without a mother, and with a drunken, absent father.

Brendan was no exception to these family rules; he had to suffer my parents' indifference or unintentional neglect too. At least that is what he told me.

"Just because I was the youngest," he said, "you think I had it better than you. But I didn't, Michael."

There is a phenomenon in my family—perhaps it is indigenous to all big families—that each person thinks his or her life is harder than all the other lives. But I don't think that is what Brendan meant. He literally meant, I think, that the youngest sibling's life is no better or worse than anyone else's.

That was the similarity we had: hard times were shared. But differences existed too, to be sure. He was fair and blond and I was dark and had blackish brown hair. I was tall—at least for people in my family—and he was average height. I was kind of big, and though he was well built, he was not big. He was decidedly blue-collar and working-class; I had my aspirations toward a literary life, teaching and writing books. But in recent years, I have been joined to my family by our common addiction to alcohol and other drugs, then by recovery.

We both loved to play paddleball too. Though Brendan was the better athlete and certainly the better paddleball player, I managed to beat him when we played by the intimidation factor of an older brother. I knew how to psych him out. I had the advantage of getting him riled, distracted, out of his game. I remember that my brother Peter, nowhere near me as a basketball player, nonetheless was able to beat me regularly at the Cross Street School courts because he was my older brother and knew how to get under my skin, bug me, and make me lose my focus.

Brendan had been the superjock in our family, one of the best baseball players our little town had known. The living- and dining-rooms' cabinets were filled with his trophies. I had only one trophy in my life, that one for basketball, the year I went an entire season without missing a foul shot, though I had long ago misplaced the gold-laminated figure on a wooden base. I had also earned a scholar's letter in grammar school, not a scarlet A, but a green-and-gold one, the colors of Saint Aidan's, and instead of a basketball or football on the letter, there was an emblazoned scholar's lamp. That, too, had long ago been misplaced.

You did not keep objects long in a big family. I remember once accumulating a small box full of Indianhead pennies and buffalohead nickels. One day, it vanished. I learned that Brendan, a small boy, had dipped into the coin supply to buy candy and gum, not knowing that these pennies and nickels were worth more than their face value. But, of course, I had done similar things to my older brothers, borrowing Peter's favorite sport jacket and ruining it at a party, and loaning myself Jimmy's Duke Ellington album, only to put a big scratch in it.

As my youngest brother slept, I got up, and instead of

drinking coffee, eating breakfast, or reading a newspaper, I decide to go for a run. I figure that running will calm me and that, given the day, I will need to stay calm. I cannot recall the last time all of us were together in one place, and that thought puts me on edge. Even two years earlier, during the fiftieth-anniversary celebration for my parents, a few siblings were missing-in-action.

I put on a pair of nylon shorts, white socks, a T-shirt, and my new cross-training athletic shoes, the ones I bought the day before at the factory outlet with Joe. The shoes feel good, though they do not give off that luxurious feeling that new running shoes—more expensive than these cross-training shoes—offer. Cross-trainers are better than sneakers, though. So they aren't running shoes. Still, they feel good. They would do just fine for a short run of five or so slow miles along the deserted beach. I tiptoe around the room, go to the door, open it, and slip down the hall without waking Brendan, though he does grunt and mumble as I stand by the door, about to reach for the knob.

It is early enough in the morning and deep enough in the off-season so that the roadway and the beach parking lots and the beaches themselves are quite empty, and I enjoy the desolate seacoast feeling it gives off. I like resorts in off-season when they are empty of people and commerce.

I trot along the roadway, then into several big parking lots, sometimes going onto the walkways on the beach that are covered by drifting sand. When the beach sand is hard enough, I run on that too, though I am going so slow, to call it running is a misnomer. I really move somewhere between a jog and a walk, taking in the new scenery. The only other time I have been here—during the fiftieth anniversary—I was in and out of Florida in a flash. I flew down, attended the party, and flew back the next day to New York. This would be different. I would be here for nearly a week. And though I had planned to continue my irrational dislike of Florida, I actually find the deserted parking lots and beaches quite appealing.

Frequently, women running with big dogs—a Doberman, a German shepherd, and a rottweiler—pass me. Sometimes the runners come toward me, then quickly shoot past. Other times, they come from behind, say hello, and move quickly on with their dogs trotting along beside them. Once, a tiny woman with a greyhound passed me too. That's when I thought of my sister Rosemary because she recovers greyhounds that have outlived their racing days and whose lives are about to be terminated. She and her husband, Paul, a deaf printer, take them back to their house. They had done this in New York and continued the practice in Florida, so they always have one or two greyhounds in their charge.

My new cross-training athletic shoes start to hurt my feet. They pinch my little toe on the right foot. I stop jogging and walk. The humidity makes the sweat ride on the surface of my skin. I think about a shower in a little while. I remember once again why I am here. It is not to see my sisters or my mother, nor to see my brothers. I have come to Clearwater to bury my father. No amount of exercise or well-being negates that fact. He was born; he lived; he died. In between, he married; he made sixteen children; nine of them lived. I was one of those fertilized eggs. How sad it all seems because we are almost interchangeable and insignificant, made to feel that we are not unique.

Neighbors and teachers tended to group my kin together as "that family." Some people were even offended that there were so many of us. In fact, that is probably what offended them the most: the overwhelming number of us. Perhaps our numbers—and how similar we looked—threatened their fragile sense of self and self-worth. Besides the number, we were an urban family that had moved to the suburbs and that had lessened its chances by drugs and alcohol. While the numbers scared the neighbors and the non-Catholic teachers we had—the Catholic ones thought our parents virtuous, even saintly, for not practicing birth control—I believe that my parents thought the number of children they had would lessen the odds of doing poorly on Long Island. After all, one or two of them might succeed quite well. Besides, we were gifted children, if not motivated to succeed; certainly even though we were not encouraged to excel, we had vivid imaginations of success where all others might fail. No wonder people did not like us and even thought we were dangerous. In some respects, our commune was worse than being Communists; we did not honor the sacred values of hard work and earning money. We were aesthetes amid the tasteless swirl of Long Island and the suburbs. I suppose this bohemian side of my family is what I found most attractive about them. We were like Henry Miller in Paris before we even heard of him.

More women runners with large dogs pass me. Sweat pours off me. Even though it is not warm, it is humid. I run along the beach for what I guess to be two and a half miles—I am running twelve-minute miles, a snail's pace, for about half an hour—and then I turn around and come back toward the motel where we are staying. I am looking forward to going upstairs and taking a long, hot shower, shaving, and getting ready to face the day. I get back to the motel dripping wet, because the sweat has not evaporated off my skin.

When I return to my room, I smell coffee and see three of my brothers smoking, kibitzing, and eating donuts, and then I discover as I go to take a shower that there is no hot water. I come out of the bathroom wearing a towel, agitated and annoyed. I call the front desk. That's when I find out that there would be no hot water for several days. The boiler has broken. Right as we speak on the telephone, plumbers are outside removing the broken boiler. They are the very people who woke me earlier in the morning, and they still struggle to get the rusted boiler onto the truck.

The kid on the telephone was surly and indifferent, even when I told him that I needed to get a shower in order to go to a funeral. Maybe he thought I was kidding. If I wasn't yet in one of my famous—I should say *our* famous—Stephens rages, I had this furious simmering low-downness about me, this quality that I was not going to take crap from anyone today. So I go downstairs, not with the intention of getting in a fight—after all, I get into fights with people, verbally and physically, even when I have no intention of getting into a fight—but rather with the purpose of clearing up our predicament. The others had not run five miles on a humid beach, but they still need to shower and get ready for the funeral. I am going to ask for the manager and I am not going to mince words or beat about the bush or take no for an answer; I am not going to take any of his grief, his gruff, his bullshit, his scheming and conniving. I want a shower. After that, dressed somberly in a dark suit with a white shirt and a tie, I would wait with dignity, just the way I had always heard people behaved when attending a funeral.

As I descend to the lobby to confront the surly desk clerk, I think to myself, not so much about the hot water being off but about funerals. Our family—poor and crazy and sick—had not really had that many funerals. I have been to only a handful of them in my life, and already I am a middle-aged man. In some respects, I'm quite lucky.

But I am back to the world of the living.

"Why didn't you at least put up a sign in the lobby?" I ask the clerk at the front desk of the Econolodge motel. "You should have done that."

He says nothing and goes in the back, I'm not sure why, maybe to get the manager or a gun to shoot me. My paranoia is racing ahead of me.

The manager comes out looking equally annoyed with me.

"We've got to go to a funeral in an hour," I tell him.

Still, the manager does not budge, looking at me as if I were a termite or, keeping with the tropical motif, a gecko.

Suddenly, I grow dark inside. The feeling I must be giving off is like a tropical depression, that uncomfortable feeling one gets before a storm. The manager picks up on it immediately. I do not threaten him, do not give him a dirty look. Yet he senses a change in me, and he responds to it. I tell him that we are not going to pay our motel bill because we paid for a room with hot water and hadn't received a room with hot water, only a room and nothing more.

"Whattaya want me to do?" the manager asks.

"We're going to go to another motel to shower," I respond.

"What?" he asks, flabbergasted.

"I've got to go to a funeral," I say again.

The college kid at the desk shrugs his shoulders as if to say, *Yankees, what can you do about them?* The manager grunts, as if, shotgun in hand, he would have blown me away.

"I've got to go to my *father's* funeral," I now add, and this time it registers. My father has died, and we have to get to the funeral, and suddenly the manager turns white, then red, then pale white again.

"I'm sorry," the manager says.

But I know it is too late for apologies.

He goes on, "Let me pay for everything."

Now it is my turn to ask, "What?"

"Everything," he repeats.

"Everything?" I ask.

"Yes," he says, nodding.

What he means, I think, is that he is not going to charge us for the night before and that he will put us up in another motel for free. I ponder his proposal for a few seconds, nod my head in agreement without saying a word, and then turn on my heels and walk away. I walk out of his office, my shoulders hunched up, smoldering in my familial rage, almost frustrated at his lack of argument until I get on the elevator and realize that he has offered to pay for our motel rooms for the rest of our stay in Florida. When I get off the elevator, I have a bounce in my step that is totally inappropriate in our situation. I try to be more solemn, but I cannot be solemn. I put the key in the door lock, then knock on the door, and step into the room where three of my brothers are engaged in an animated discussion about pancakes.

"Blueberry are best."

"No, asshole, buckwheat with bananas."

"Hey, fuckface, how about strawberry pancakes?"

Once the discussion of pancakes ends, all of them get moody, each complaining about the lack of hot water. I repeat what has happened downstairs, but it does not sink in yet. *Give it time,* I think, and pack my bags to leave the motel. Seeing me pack, one by one, Joe, then Brendan, and finally Tom gets the message and packs too.

As we check out of the Econolodge—bags and persons in morning disarray—Tom stands by the exit doing nothing. He lingers in the doorway, something he does well, if not exquisitely. Brendan demands that Tom grab a few suitcases and toss them in the van. Tom balks. You cannot tell him to do anything. Put another way: everything related to Tom is a complication. One of them shoves the other. The next thing I know they are going at each other, no longer verbally, but physically, like cats and dogs. Like World War III just broke out.

Joe and I separate them.

I tell Brendan, "Get a grip."

"Cool it," Joe says to Tommy.

Still, I can't be too shocked. Peter and I carried on like this when we were kids. But, of course, we were kids then, not middle-aged guys acting like teenagers. Shouldn't they at least behave differently on the day of their father's funeral? Or perhaps this kind of behavior is exactly what the Chief wanted and deserved, a clan of bickering sons, pounding each other into dust in an Econolodge lobby.

I become impressed by the fact that I have not blown up, have not lost my cool. Instead of walking away with the Pyrrhic victory of a pugilist, I come away with the real victory of a diplomat; I got what I set out to get and more, and I had not behaved badly, something all of us slipped into too easily, especially now, the day of the funeral, when it is almost de rigueur to behave poorly. At least I know that I am capable of such behavior in a heartbeat—at the drop of a hat.

I am now ready to move to the new digs.

Joe stands in the lobby and grouses about the move, while I have become intensely quiet. Once again, Brendan and Tommy go at each other, most of it having to do with Tom literally not carrying his share of the load. Now they are in each other's face, shouting and pointing fingers and on the verge of more blows. One of the bags breaks and Brendan asks Tom to pick it up, but Tom refuses, feels put-upon, as if he were being used, even though all of us are carrying bags and trying to make the most of a bad situation.

"You scumbag bum," Brendan shouts, "pick up the fucking clothes."

"You pick it up," Tom shouts back. "I'm your older brother."

"Big deal," Brendan says, sneering.

Then Tom shouts, "Hey, listen, you can't talk to me like that."

"Why not?"

"I'm older than you."

I remember my older brother Peter saying this only the day before at my mother's.

"If you're my older brother, how come I'm always taking care of you, paying your bills and feeding you, letting you sleep at my house for free?"

Joe had told me that the last time Tom had stayed at Brendan's was when the Nassau police had pulled up to the house, dumping Tom at the doorstep. He had told the police—when they picked him up drunk, roaming the streets at four in the morning—that Brendan's house was where he lived. Brendan told the cops not to leave him there, that Tom did not live with him. But it had become a domestic matter, a family affair, and rather than listen to Brendan, they told him to work it out with his brother, and then they left.

With Brendan in the frontseat, Joe manages to get Tom in the backseat of the van. We drive off to the new motel.

The new digs are a few blocks in from the shore, down a crowded street of mom-and-pop motels painted in gaudy colors, treeless but often with swimming pools out front and colored lights ready to shine on the buildings at night. It does not feel like the 1990s but rather the 1950s, if not innocent, then at least naive. A tacky beauty pervades everything. The decor is so gauche that, on the day of my father's funeral, it looks just right, almost too perfect.

Now the brother combatants fall silent, separated by two other brothers and several benches in the van. We have managed to escape the hot-waterless Econolodge for the Blue Jay, a mom-and-pop operation on the back shore, down a tacky row of tightly squeezed together, economy-class motels. Our hosts are a young Polish couple full of condolences and well-wishing who are not quite prepared for the gruffness of the so-called mourning brothers. Joe is a great joker, and he has been on a roll since we met up at Kennedy Airport two days earlier. As with any group of males without women, the dirty jokes pour out of us, and somehow, even before we get to the Blue Jay Motel where the Polish couple is, Joe and Brendan are talking about, for reasons that are unfathomable, Polish vaginas. They decide to call it *pronsky,* one of them claiming that as its slang name in Polish. So it is pronsky this and pronsky that, as we have breakfast or drive around in the van, and as we pull up to the motel, pronsky comes flying out of their mouths. Of course, the hosts, being Polish, then become Mr. and Mrs. Pronsky, or the Pronskys, for short. So instead of these four dour brothers who need to shower and get ready for a father's funeral, the Polish couple meets a van full of laughing brothers, brothers rolling and sliding, whacking each other on the back, screaming at the top of their lungs, "Oh, my God, it's the Pronskys," or, "The Blue Jay is full of pronsky, man, wait and see," or Joe, the best mimic among us, affecting my father's voice, "I'll give ya a pronsky, ya crazy little bastard ya!"

Eventually we calm down, and once I get showered, step into a dark suit, white shirt, tie, and dress shoes and socks, the somber mood descends like a bad case of depression over my head and shoulders and down my back, clear to my ankles. When I see my three brothers in dark suits, I want to cry, only I have lost any ability to cry, so instead I have this case of sinus trouble, a pain in my nose as if I had eaten ice cream too quickly, swollen hurting eyes, sniffles, and a dry mouth. So do the brothers. All of us collectively take to wearing sunglasses on this sunless, glareless, overcast breezy November morning.

The couple sees that we really are four brothers down here, indeed, for our father's funeral, down here and down and out, out of sorts, down and dirty, with those mean blues that be coming with death. We all have a bad case of the Clearwater blues, which is not a fish, nor the color of water, nor a cerulean sky. This is an old broken-down feeling, like wearing a beat-up old jacket on a hot, humid day. It is like whistling into the wind as you walk along a train track. We have come down to mourn our father, a terrible old fellow, a man who lived a life and now is gone. He is gone gone, like they sang. He is gone like a turkey through the corn.

III.

7

The Amends

As the Druid Chapel fills up with mourners, I see my oldest brother, Jimmy, across the room. He is surrounded by an entourage of stepchildren, a new son, wife, and friends. In the front of the chapel sits my sister Kaitlin, regally being attended to because she can't walk after a knee operation. There, too, is my sister Peggy, the second youngest of the clan, now a wife and mother herself, her husband and daughter at her side. Peter, toothless, suited, wearing cowboy boots, bearded and, like all of us brothers, bald, greets the guests. Joe, along with Tommy and Brendan, sits in the back talking to relatives and friends, accepting condolences, even—being who we are—cracking jokes. The only thing missing, as in the old days, is a bar complete with whiskey and a keg of beer and wine for the ladies. This would be a dry occasion in the funeral parlor: no tears, no booze, no regrets, thank you.

All of us are glad to see our father leave the mortal place for whatever lay beyond this one. But each probably has a different reason for his leave-taking being auspicious. The kinder, more forgiving siblings look upon his last years as too full of suffering, so that death was a release from that chain of misery. The more bitter among us—I lean toward the bitter roots—are simply glad he is gone, that he no longer can bother us. Yet I have my doubts about the veracity of that observation. I feel that my father will be with me until my own end and maybe even beyond that; he might lurk in the corners forever, ghost, free spirit, idea, malediction, evil possibility, or weak desire. The three sisters—oh, Moscow!—seem the most balanced between grief and recrimination. The two older brothers seem the most upset, and the younger brothers seem, not indifferent, not overly bitter, but not so emotionally charged either. What I realize, seeing my father earlier, is that I had never really resolved my differences with him, even if he resolved his own differences with me. In fact, I recall the telephone conversation—at the time I thought it just another innocuous one from my family—in which I think he made his amends to me.

He spoke to me of his strokes shortly after I had been released from Smithers, an alcohol and drug treatment facility in Manhattan. In that telephone conversation, he told me that he was in a group—I, too, was an outpatient in aftercare, but at Roosevelt Hospital's alcohol treatment facility—for stroke patients and that the leader of the group was teaching them to let go and let God, to turn it over, to admit their powerlessness and the unmanageability of their illnesses. He told me that he had come to accept that his own life would not get much better than what it was at that moment, that he would continue to have strokes and eventually he would get much worse. I had forgotten this conversation until that moment—really moments after seeing my father in the casket—when it came back to me, not from seeing him moments earlier but from seeing my brothers and sisters troop into the chapel, seeing my mother putting on a good face, putting her Catholic spin on it—"He's gone to his resting place in Heaven." That's when it came back to me that even if I had not made amends to my father, he had attempted to make them to me.

And I had things to make amends for. If I couldn't remember them, my siblings would help me. Jimmy comes over to say hello and introduce some of his friends. When the friends move away, he asks me, "You see Ron anymore?" He is speaking of an old, dear college friend whom I had not seen in many years until quite recently.

"He's sober," I say.

"Sober?" Jimmy asks. "I didn't know Ron had a drinking problem."

"How could he be my friend and not have a drinking problem?" I ask.

"True," he says. Then my oldest brother reminds me of that time I had the fight with the old man in the backyard after Ron had come by for a visit.

I had dropped out of college, and that first summer back home is when it happened. My family thought I had dropped out because of a heart condition, and in fact some tests at Saint Francis, a heart hospital on Long Island, suggested some damage, though the tests did not determine the cause. Of course, I had a good idea what the problem was because I had been drinking and drugging like crazy since I first went to college, and suddenly my high-life living had caught up to my body and was delivering a punishing blow to my liver and heart and everything else. I was recuperating at home, but home on Long Island was not a peaceful place in those days. My mother actively drank her bottles of gin and gallons of wine; Jimmy had been discharged from the military on mental grounds; Peter was in trouble in the neighborhood; the younger children were not doing well in school; the old man was at the height of his own madness, this combination of workaholism and alcoholism, obligation to family and aversion to the clan. Still, he would come home to this nucleus of dissension, railing and carrying on about what a bunch of bums his sons and daughters were.

I made the mistake of inviting my friend Ron, a classmate from college, over to the house to read some new poems and a play I had written. Ron was an old friend by now, himself a Long Islander, a former all-American lacrosse player, and a big drinking and drugging buddy, not to mention a fellow poet and writer. My friend had brought over a bottle of wine. After reading the poems, we sat in the cluttered, noisy, dirty, chaotic living room of our house to read the play. My mother had herself a glass of the wine from the bottle that Ron had brought over; so did I and a few other siblings. We smoked cigarettes, and as the wine was quaffed, we decanted the words of my play. Then my father walked in the door after a rotten day in Hell's Kitchen.

"What's going on here?" he screamed, seeing my friend Ron with his Gauloises cigarettes stinking up the room and his half-gallon jug of wine and me and my mother and siblings sitting around reading parts to the play. "Who the hell are you?"

Ron reached out to shake my father's hand. Though I had warned him about my father in the past and would not have invited him over to the house if I had thought the old man was going to be home early, I know that Ron did not expect what was to follow.

"Get out!" my father screamed.

Ron, like myself, had long hair and a beard, dungarees and a blue chambray workshirt, and a nice pair of leather sandals he bought on West Fourth Street in the Village— shaggy and beat and very un–civil servant in his manner. He spoke in this high-thespian way that would annoy a civil servant from Brooklyn. In so many words, he was, like me, my father's enemy.

"Out!" my father screamed, like King Lear on the cliffs.

"But we were just reading Michael's play," pleaded Ron.

"Michael?" my father asked. "Who's Michael? I don't have any son named Michael."

"Now wait a minute," Ron said, as my father, dropping any further pretense toward conversation, began to shove my friend toward the door.

"You're all a bunch of bums. You ought to be drafted into the military, get decent haircuts, and learn to become adults!" shouted the old man.

"Don't push," Ron said.

"You can't push him," I shouted, feeling the wine shoot right to my head. "He's my best friend."

The next thing I knew Ron was outside, the wine bottle was broken on the stoop, the kids were shouting and crying, my mother was pleading with my father and me to stop, and we were going at each other in the front yard.

This was a rite of passage with my father, one which I found onerous and which I vowed never to be a part of. My other brothers had to go out into the yard with him at some point too. All the neighbors stopped cutting their lawns, attending to their barbecues, washing their windows, and stared at us fighting in the front yard, father and son or, more accurately, father and another one of his sons, fighting and clawing and shoving and punching. Other neighbors stared out their windows, shaking their heads at what an awful family we were.

I once heard a neighbor say, "That family reduces the value of the entire community with their outrageous behavior."

I thought of myself, if not as good a fighter as some of my brothers, then at least a good boxer. Jimmy and Peter had created myths and legends about their fighting in and outside the family, particularly Jimmy who was genuinely big and tough. Me, I boxed, not something that made for legend, but I knew how to defend myself. I kept my father away from me with a stiff jab, not wanting to engage him. But he was out to do real damage, pouring on his roundhouse, barroom punches. He was, as almost always, freewheeling and dangerous. He had his head down and bore into me, and I sidestepped him almost like a matador evading a bull, only our arena of action was proscribed by the privet hedges, the ailanthus tree, the brick steps, and the side of the house. He got me good a few times, mostly in the face and once or twice in the mouth. It was when he hit me in the face, humiliating me, that I blew up, my whole head and body exploding with years of rage toward my father, and suddenly Michael, the quiet one in the family, went off on his old man, hitting the father with all his might. I got him into a headlock with my left arm and pummeled his face with my right hand, and when he did something nasty to break my hold, we went back to punching each other until one of my punches took the starch out of him and disabled his aggression. The next thing I knew I had my hands around my father's huge neck and I was strangling him, if not to death (though that was a potential, I admit now) then to unconsciousness. His face turned several shades, from pale white to beet red to a sickly blue-green, as the breath was strangled out of him by his third-oldest son in the front yard as the children and wife and neighbors and my friend Ron all looked on horrified at what Michael—"the nicest of all the Stephens boys," an older neighbor had said—was doing to the old man.

Okay, okay, I imagined a neighbor saying. *The father treated those kids badly, and he probably deserved everything that Michael did to him, but that was his son out there strangling him like that in front of all the neighbors, strangling him and not stopping once he saw that the father had been disengaged and was no longer a threat, that the fight had ended and the steam had gone out of the old man while the rage in the third-oldest boy seemed to boil further over.*

I jumped into Ron's Cadillac Coupe de Ville, his mother's car, a Great Neck car, a mafioso's car, a Hempstead pimp's car, a big-time gambler at the golf course car, only two bearded hippies sat in it, and we drove over to Ron's house in Valley Stream on the South Shore. Williston Park had no Coupe de Villes; it only had Dodge Darts and other midrange items from Detroit on its streets.

My friend was more upset than I was. All I had done was confront the inevitable; I had gone through an ugly ritual that everyone in my family experienced. Fighting in the backyard with the old man was a rite of passage in our family, particularly for the brothers. You solemnly went into the yard with the old man after words were said in the house. Then he went after you physically, and you had better defend yourself or, better yet, go on the offensive, kick ass and take names later.

Ron drove the car onto the Meadowbrook Parkway a few towns away and then pointed the Cadillac south in the direction of his family's house.

"I can't believe that you were doing that to your own father," Ron said, still incredulous at what he had witnessed.

"I'll kill the fucker," I fumed, I steamed, I agitated. "If he ever bothers me again, I'll kill him."

So I stayed at Ron's for a while, and then he got a place in the city and I found a place to stay with my brother Peter who worked as a stagehand then, the apartment on East Forty-ninth Street. Outside of this apartment one night, Peter found a menstruating woman walking around naked. Lady Godiva of Second Avenue we called her. Peter brought her back to the apartment. Things like that happened at the apartment regularly. Eventually I found work in the fall at the new Lincoln Center music library, getting an apartment on the Lower East Side, and not going back to Long Island for many years after that.

I didn't even know how to make the amends to my father for that evening a lifetime ago. All I could do—in the absence of booze and overrun with new and old feelings and primordial emotions—was experience that mental and physical state once again and say a prayer that God forgave me because, if my father was cognizant of my thoughts wherever he was, I know he still did not forgive me and probably still did not wish me well, though I could just be hedging my bets by saying this. My father was a fighter himself, and since he expected each one of his sons to go out into the yard and have it out, perhaps he forgave me a long time ago, figuring that even his bookish son Michael could handle himself with his fists now. The truth of the matter is that from that age until I was about twenty-six years old, bookish or not, I had more fights with people than I care to remember or admit to, though thankfully I had not had any for the past twenty years or more, no doubt a blow to my father's esteem for his pugilistic sons, but a blessing in disguise because each time I fought, something dirty and evil rose up inside of me, sickening me even as it created that momentary exhilaration which fighting provided. The real amends I would make to my father for that fight would be this: this sentence, this paragraph, these chapters and words, this book, those memories, the curl and twist of a paragraph winding down the page, the intricacy of a sentence boxed in by other ornamentations of words and grammar, the strobe light of memory working the production, that burst of feeling which propelled the words onward, the groan of emotions, rocking from the heels upward through the spine and into the head, exploding out of the ears and tongue and eyes and from the nostrils and out of the fingertips, this homage, I mean, this utterance, this literary pulse would be my amends to the old man.

8

The Gratitude

On the drive back to the motel, Joe, Brendan, and I talk about drive-by shootings, particularly in recent months in Florida. I realize that, like me, my brothers are tense. All three of us are very short with Tommy, his thick-headedness especially annoying this evening; I want to grab him in a headlock, like when we were kids, and deliver a barrage of noogies to his head until he gets the message to shut up and stop bothering us with his endless questions and his saying how he's going to turn his life around, how he had a harder life than all of us—Peter sometimes likes to talk like this too—though for the life of me I can't understand how our lives were any easier than theirs.

Everything annoys me this evening. I have a great big "fuck-it" attitude. I say to my brothers in short order: it is too muggy outside; I'm tired; everyone's getting on my nerves; what's the point of all this nonsense about an open-casket funeral; I wish I hadn't come down; I wish I were not a part of this family; I wish I had never been born.

"Is there anything good about your life?" Joe asks while driving through traffic in the white rental van.

"What do you mean?" I ask.

"You've been bitching and moaning since we left Mom's condo," Brendan says.

"Yeah," Joe says, "don't you have any gratitude, man? You

know, a grateful heart will never drink and all that good stuff."

Sometimes alcoholic slogans drive me to want a drink. But I see his point. I understand the gist of what he is saying. I'm setting myself up for a big fall. I'm letting the disease isolate me from everyone. Once it has me there, it will invite me to dance with it, flirting all the while. The next thing I know I'll be drunk. Alcoholism is not a subtle disease. I have heard it referred to as cunning and baffling, but I prefer the description of it being rapacious.

"Aren't you grateful for anything?" Joe asks again.

"No," I say, but they know I am kidding from the way I answer him.

"Well, I have a beautiful daughter," I say.

"There you go," Brendan chimes in.

"I've got my health," I say.

"Minus our rotten Stephens teeth," Joe says.

"Let's not get into the teeth," I say because I recently had my seventh or eighth operation on my jaw and gums and teeth. So has Joe. In fact, I think he's had more dental operations than I have had.

"What else?" Brendan asks.

"I've got a book coming out in a few months," I say.

"You didn't drink today," Joe says.

"True," I answer. "I haven't had a drink, and if we get home soon, and I can lie down and get through Jay's or David's monologue, it will be ten to twelve, and then I think I will have made another day sober."

"How much time?" Brendan asks.

"Me," I say, thinking, "I have . . ."

"Five years," Joe says.

"You have more than five years," Brendan says.

"No," Joe answers him. "I mean Michael has five years now."

Brendan had some time under his belt too.

"Welcome home," I say.

"Yeah," Joe goes, "welcome home."

"Yeah," Brendan says, laughing.

Joe drives in silence for a time; then I ask him: "Isn't there anything to be grateful for?"

"No," Joe says, but he cannot keep a straight face and so laughs.

Having this conversation I realize that each of us feels disconnected from the family in similar ways. I thought my own separation from the clan was unique. But hanging out with my brothers I understand that we all feel this way.

Tom talks to himself in the last seat of the van, oblivious to anything the three of us have been talking about.

Joe parks the van and we go into our fifties wonderland motel near the water, Joe a few doors over with Tommy, while Brendan and I adjourn to our room, me to watch David Letterman and try to read, him to smoke cigarettes and read the bound galleys of my new novel, laughing his head off where other readers might cry and curse or nod their heads with literary approval. Finally, the first day of the funeral over with, lights out, I stare at the ceiling.

Usually I do an inventory of my day as I lie in bed trying to locate sleep. I am lucky that insomnia never plagued me too often as I got sober. Most evenings, I put my head to the pillow, and in the midst of doing the inventory of my day, I fall asleep. When I wake in the morning, quite often off the beam in terms of my own sobriety, I need to get to a meeting as soon as I can. But this evening, before I even do the inventory, I recall how I drifted through the entire day without too much gratitude. This orphaned feeling that arises when I am with my family overtook me both in the funeral parlor's chapel and at an Irish pub the family went to for dinner. There was a lot of "poor me, poor me, pour me a drink" in my day. More than once I asked, "Why was I born, God? Why was I born into this family?"

Brendan mumbles in his sleep in the bed next to mine. It reminds me of when I was a kid, sleeping on the porch of our tiny house in a giant-sized bed that just fit into the corner. On one side slept Jimmy; on the other, Peter. Invariably one of them had a dream during the night that turned me into some pleasant object next to them. I'd wake with an arm draped over me. If they woke like this, I would get punched. If they slept, I was stuck for the night this way, afraid to move because I didn't want to get punched one last time before sunrise.

How much have they changed since those days? I have to say, a lot and not at all. It reminds me of a few hours earlier, walking back to the chapel after dinner. Everyone discussed whose car they were going back in from the restaurant to the funeral parlor. I finally asked Peter if he wanted to walk. As I close my eyes in bed, I see him walking with me back to the funeral parlor. I walk back about a half mile to the funeral parlor in the thick humid air. I am with my brother Peter who is anxious about where his children are. Over a lifetime, I have been in an on-and-off friendship with Peter. Presently it is off. The last time I saw him in New York City was that day I bought him breakfast and he lectured me afterward about what was wrong with me. Shortly after that he buzzed out of town to Florida. He hasn't picked up a drink or a drug for a year.

I recall his telephone conversation with me the week before our father died. Immediately he went into his presumptions; he presumed, right away, that I would not come to the funeral. I had been so vocal about how much I disliked the Chief. I had no gratitude, Peter said. Still, I explained to him, "It's my father you're talking about," trying to hold back the indignation. "Of course I'll come down for the funeral." I had no gratitude, Peter said. But I did have gratitude.

Seeing Jimmy and Peter earlier in the day reminded me of when we were children. They stood in the front of the chapel, speaking with friends and relatives, acting like the heads of a crime family. My two older brothers made me think of the Katzenjammer Kids, that comic strip with two mischievous boys. The Katzenjammers (their name means "hangover" in German or "the yowling of cats") even had black and blond heads of hair like my two brothers. Hans and Fritz were the comic-strip characters' names.

Hans and Fritz make a giant firecracker to blow up the Captain.

In a moment of conscience—something quite rare for these boys, either my brothers or the comic-strip brothers—the one who looks like Jimmy (Hans) says to his brother, "I almost feel ashamed of myself, Fritz!"

More often they did things like let a goat eat all the books in their house while Fritz (Peter) says, "A good book should be vell digested!"

Though Jimmy and I have been close, he had an odd response to my writing. Two years ago, when I visited Florida for the first time, while driving to the airport, his wife asked me about my first novel.

"Jimmy won't tell me anything about it," she said.

Before I could say anything, he answered for me, "That was a long time ago; we don't need to discuss that book anymore."

Yet since I got sober myself, Jimmy has warmed up to me. He has become more willing to talk on the telephone if I call. I say "if I call" because I don't remember him ever calling me about anything, even in those terminal days with my father.

Peter was more the big brother in that regard. He liked to give advice. He liked to *call* me to give advice. Somehow, he believed, no matter what my circumstances and his were, that I needed help. I was naive; I had no real street experience like he did.

So I lingered around my sisters and my mother because my other brothers, the ones I came down to Florida with, are in the back of the chapel talking with their nephews, joking and laughing.

I came from the back of the room to say hello to my sister Kaitlin. She looked so regal in the front of the chapel because she is unable to walk. Her knees had been replaced, so she had to sit in a strategic spot in the front row of mourners, greeting anyone who came by to say hello. Her crutches lay beside her. She could not stand. Relatives bent to kiss her, say hello, and offer their best wishes.

Alexandra, Peggy and Ricardo's daughter, like all the nieces in the family, is a young beauty, and because she is so young and knows nothing about death, she thinks it is a party and how funny that Grandpa is up there sleeping. Should she go up and wake up Grandpa?

"No, dear," my mother told her, "let Grandpa sleep."

My mother—though she is supposed to be the poor widow who sits in the front of the room and whom everyone walks up to in order to offer their condolences—is forever the caretaker; she runs around, making sure that everyone is all right.

"Are you all right, dear?" mother asked.

It does not matter if you are young or old, her child, grandchild, or no relation at all. My mother calls you "dear."

"I'm okay," I said.

"You look pale," she observed.

"I live in New York City," I said. "There's no sunlight in the winter and I don't get outside enough."

"And you?" she asked Brendan. "Are you all right, dear?"

"Yeah, sure," he said, sounding like the truck driver that he is.

"And you?" she asked Joe.

"What?" Joe asked.

"Are you all right, dear?"

"Of course I'm all right," Joe answered. "Why wouldn't I be all right, Rosie?"

We often call her Rosie when we want to tease her. But

we have called her Rosie for so long, she does not respond to the name.

"I just want to be sure you're all right, dear," she said, and checked on another set of relations across the room.

I went to the back of the room and played with Jimmy's son Drew; then I talked with my nephew Dustin about New York, said hello to more members of the family, and every once in a while, I found myself looking at my father in the front of the Druid Chapel. A knot wrapped itself around my stomach's lining. Self-pity and low self-esteem soaked me like a sweat. I have no gratitude. I have no gratitude, it is true. I am without gratitude. When I am in this mood, I often think, *He never loved any of us.* Of course, Mom says, when any of us bring up this touchy subject, that he loved each one of us in his own *special* way. That's why her simple, uncomplicated kind of love is so important; she had to provide the love of two parents for nine children while making beds, sweeping, and making endless meals for the demanding prima donnas that all her children were. Some households produced prodigies; our family had a knack for turning out prodigal children.

I get out of bed and go to the bathroom. Brendan snores in his bed. I can hear Tommy talking loudly from a few doors down the hall. I also hear Joe say, annoyed, "Go to bed, man." When I get back into bed, I return to thoughts of the preceding day, trying to make sense of it. I think back to the conversation with Joe and Brendan about gratitude. And I remember my father. Do I have any gratitude for him? I am not sure. That's what keeps me awake. I remember when I was eighteen years old, a sophomore in college, and the old man finally made a connection for me to get Seaman's Papers. I capitalize these words because they were that important to my life, catapulting me from a New York provincial into someone who went off to sea and experienced the world. Those papers were going to expand my universe tenfold. But the problem with getting them was a bit of a Kafka-like dilemma. You had to have a ship willing to take you on in order to get Seaman's Papers, and the only way to get a ship to take you on was if you had the papers already. That is where my father came in.

My father wanted to let me know that he had connections up and down the waterfront. I should have been grateful to him. Not grateful. That is not what I mean. He wanted me to be beholden to him. But he wanted me to sweat a little too. Peter had stiffed him the year before when the old man had gotten him a job as a bursar on a ship, even picked up a spiffy uniform. Then my brother jumped off in the ship's first port of call—Norfolk, Virginia. So I persisted in my request, explaining to him that I was not Peter. Finally my father gave in because it allowed him to be a big shot but also because the sea was in our blood. His family had come from the west coast of Ireland, traditionally a seafaring region. My mother's grandfather had published a magazine about the sea, its commerce, and the economy of the great harbor. Her brother Bill, my uncle Billy, had been murdered on a ship off of Pusan, Korea, during the war, and his body was never recovered. But a detail such as Uncle Billy's disappearance did not necessarily lessen my chances of getting the papers. Perhaps the sea needed another one of us to be offered up to it. With his connections on the waterfront, my father made telephone calls that got me a letter from a shipping company that I took down to the old Custom House at Bowling Green. I got my Seaman's Papers, and within a few months, I shipped out on the SS *Independence*.

Even in the quiet motel room near the water, I still hear the prodigious noise that my family made throughout the day. Grief was not a soft, delicate, private experience for them. The noise that emanated from my family was extraordinary, like a giant animal in its lair, talking to its own shadow. I now understand what attracted Kelts to bagpipes. It is not talk but skirls that I hear, the jigs and reels and dirges of the pipes flattening out in the humid air. It drowned out the country jukebox and even the noisy drunks at the ersatz Irish bar where we had dinner.

In the lobby of the funeral parlor, I heard one of the junior assistant funeral directors allude to the fact that the funeral in the Druid was one of the noisiest he had ever heard.

A large, older southern man, his face pasty and full of that professional insincerity of undertakers, said, "That's the way the Irish are at funerals."

"But these are noisier than any Irish I ever heard," the young junior assistant said.

A din rose up from the chapel that afternoon; it was the ululation of my family mourning the dead. We did not weep, did not tell jokes. None of us knew how to sing or play musical instruments—though Tommy claimed, still, that he was a great guitarist—but we knew how to talk. But

why were we so enamored of speech? Talk filled out the
void. It was the enemy of silence. Rocks were silent, not
people. People spoke. Life for my family was one long conversation, an endless monologue until the end. You could
cut off our legs, pull out all our teeth, smash our noses to
pulp, rip out our guts, slice off our peckers and vaginas,
pummel us over the head with trash cans, but leave us our
tongues for talking, and probably we would not mind too
much. Cut out our tongues, tell us to shut up, suggest that
maybe we listen instead of talk, and we would explode into
endless, wrathful fury from here to kingdom come.

I noticed that my brother Joe was a great talker on the
airplane coming down, in the van when we drove around,
and at the motel, though in the presence of his dead father,
in the midst of his noisy family, he was as silent as a ghost,
just like I was. I nodded to him down at the end of the
table, and he nodded back.

Even in that noisy saloon, none of the big, drunken
workingmen at the bar equaled the noise that came from
this sober family at the long table. The voices rose in one
long, loud Brooklyn whir, the endless drone of the funeral
dirge, only rendered by human speech, our harsh New York
accents transplanted to Clearwater, Florida. Once food was
served—and the one waitress on duty, overworked, harried,
and distracted, took forever to bring the food—the voices
subsided into a low growl of approval. Food tamed the
beasts once again.

Tommy, as always, ate like a refugee, as if this was the
first meal he'd eaten in days or even weeks, maybe in
months, and he ordered as much as he could, several meals,

and each time, he ate with an almost drunken enthusiasm. I watched my nephew Dustin eat pizza, but all I could think about was the time when he was a boy, and one summer he and his mother had rented a house with my family in southern Vermont, and how he ate a whole bag of English muffins every morning for breakfast.

Allen, Kaitlin's husband, said, "You ought to come visit us on the east coast of Florida. It's very different from here."

"You'll like it," Kaitlin said.

Alexandra cried passionately at the end of the table.

"Don't hit her so hard," Peggy said to her husband.

"She must learn to listen," he said.

I flinched, always gun-shy about children getting spanked whether they deserved it or not.

"That's all right, dear," my mother told her granddaughter, but her tone was not convincing enough for the little girl.

Peter looked at his watch.

"I don't know where my kids are," he said. Then he explained that his son was coming from a military base in Texas while his two girls and his youngest son were driving down from their mother's house in North Carolina.

"Nothing to get drunk over," Joe said.

Peter gave him a look.

"Keep it simple," Brendan said.

As everyone spoke at once, Rosemary gestured extravagantly with her hands ("the Italian way," Jimmy says) for her deaf husband, Paul.

I had a mild headache, the kind I used to have as a kid, from the noise, the endless babble of the family.

I see these things not so much as mere images in my head, a dream, but real things that I have to be grateful for. I have to be grateful. So many people in my family, including my parents, were affected by alcohol, and many of them no longer drink. That list includes my older brothers, my mother, my sisters, my younger brothers. In fact, all of us are sober at the funeral. What a blessing! That might seem like a commonplace observation, but it really is the recounting of a miracle. None of them drank during that day. My God, it was not just amazing; it was miraculous. At plenty of times in my life, I have been in rooms garrulously peopled by my family when they were drinking—when they were drunk. I have never been in a room in all my life when everyone in my family was sober. God bless them, I pray. No one had a drink.

That's what I put at the head of my gratitude list as I drift off to sleep: no one drank today.

Tomorrow we bury my father.

9

Prayer for My Father

Three of the four brothers at the Blue Jay Motel are dressed in funeral suits and white shirts and drab ties with sensible black shoes and dark socks, showered and hair combed, shaved and ready to rumble off into the void of the Druid Chapel, the Catholic Mass at Saint Cecilia's that would be held, and then the cortege of rented limos and vans would wend their way from Clearwater to Saint Petersburg, on to the grounds of the soldiers' cemetery, my father's final resting place. There is no time to eat out, so Brendan and I drive to a McDonald's nearby and come back with breakfast specials, orange juice, and big containers of coffee. We eat outside, watching the herons and gulls poking through the clear, still water for fish. All of us eat the food except Tommy, who decides that it is beneath him.

"He's the uppitiest homeless person I ever met," I say, half in jest and half seriously.

"He's worse than that," Brendan says. "He's a fucking pain in the ass."

Oh, to hear how my brother Brendan says that word *fuck,* full of New York's working-class toughness, resentful and poetic. It is a word full of animistic fury and unbelievable magic on Brendan's tongue, each consonant and vowel delivered with a lyrical violence. My oldest brother, Jimmy, always says that people from Long Island—and

Brendan is totally Nassau County as opposed to his older brothers who are part Nassau and part Brooklyn—have a thicker New York accent than those from the boroughs. He is probably correct about that. At least, I could see—I mean hear—his point, listening to my brother Brendan. *Fucking Tommy,* he'd mumble. *Fucking son of a bitch. Who the fuck do they think they are? I'll fuck them up good. Fucking bastards. The fucking guys at the airport. The fucking guineas* (echoing his father). *The fucking Arab and Indian taxi drivers. The fucking cops and airport security. The fucking family. Yeah. The fucking family.* Because that's what it comes down to, the fucking family, all assembled here, though one of them, Tommy, pisses off his younger brother Brendan once again, and I have to be aware, though I am nearly a stranger in their midst, rarely seeing or socializing with them, that they see each other regularly, and Brendan especially has become, over the past decade or longer, Tommy's caretaker, his meal ticket and his crib, his brother confessor and soul mate. Poor Brendan. So fucking Tommy is at it again, getting under Brendan's skin. This time Tom is playing the pampered role. Who knows what it would be next? Probably one of his righteous outbreaks of religious indignation, Bible thumping and all, about how we are all damned, no matter that we don't drink, all of us curse too much, take the name of the Lord in vain, are disrespectful of our parents, do not go to church on Sundays, and so on.

"Fucking Tommy," Brendan says again as he watches Tommy disappear upstairs, not even close to being ready to go to the funeral.

"He's going to be late for his father's funeral," I say.

"Christ," responds Joe, "Tommy's going to be late for his own fucking funeral."

"Not if I can help it," Brendan says. Then he shouts up to his beleaguered older brother, "If you ain't ready in fifteen minutes, we're leaving you here, Tommy."

"That's right," I say, piping in, getting on the bandwagon because I am determined to get to the chapel before the others, to be there and be ready to serve and assist, lend a hand, and be generally useful to my mother and the rest of the family.

"Even *you*?" Tom asks me.

Et tu, Mickey?

"I thought you didn't get involved in this kind of fighting," he says.

But now I am as annoyed as any of them, all dressed and ready to go, the funeral Mass not that far off; we are ready to leave, but Tom is not ready. He still needs to smoke a few more cigarettes, get his bearings, chit chat about this and that and nothing at all, then leisurely, no matter the hour or the conditions, get ready. He comes down the stairs and begins a conversation with the Polish proprietor about the curios and knickknacks scattered around the grounds, tiny plastic gnomes, a donkey pulling a cart, plaster flamingos (nearly as flawless as the real ones in the water).

"Get ready!" Brendan shouts.

"I think your brothers want you to leave for the funeral," the proprietor says.

Tom ambles up the stairs and into his room while Brendan fumes under his breath and Joe talks about antique furniture and the cost of heating a house in upstate New York during the winter.

The brothers get into the white van, and we drive off. Joe drives; it would seem he has become the designated driver throughout our stay. As he drives, he sings aloud with Joe Cocker's "Something" on the radio. I can't help but think that my brother once looked a little like the British singer. Brendan sits in the killer seat, smoking cigarettes and looking tense in his neck and shoulders. Tom, following his own script, speaks with himself in the rear seat. I sit looking out the window blankly. Each day that I spend in Clearwater the sadness not so much washes over me as it soaks into my marrow. But it is not just sadness. I begin to see how tragic all our lives are, and just before we expire, the end is not usually graceful, painless, or artful. Perhaps I don't mean that our lives are tragic but rather pointless. Death is artless and dumb but totally democratic in that it gets everyone. There! It comes. It is here. It is among us. Smell it. Taste it. Don't even try to fathom it because it cannot be comprehended. What an insignificant little man my father was, and in turn, so am I, and so is everyone else: Napoleon, Dante, James Joyce, Caesar, Michelangelo, ashes to ashes, all fall down, everyone reduced to anonymous dust no matter who they were. Death is the only equal opportunity experience I would share with the rest of humanity. So it is not just sadness but a mood that verges on despair, and how, as I did in the past, I mask these sensations by feeling rage and anger, though this morning I am not able to conjure the hair-trigger explosion. I'm bloated by these feelings.

I also feel a specific grief that my father and I never came to any closure, much less a discovery, about our relationship. It is as if he disappeared before I could find out what was what, shout and scream, and, who knows, even come to some kind of terminal resolution, expressing our heartfelt feelings for each other while still acknowledging our differences. But this was not to be, not for me but also not for any of my brothers and sisters, because after four days in Florida, I see in ways I never saw before that I am not unique in my feelings about our father. Each one of us carries around this same baggage for a lifetime, and each one of us brought it to Clearwater, maybe expecting to air our dirty linen, though no true opportunity presents itself, no dramatic moment comes. Instead of revelations, we have our dull little aches, physical and psychic, plaguing us like an inherited arthritic condition, a pain in the little bones of the feet, an ague in the cheeks of the ass and up the lower back and down the top of the legs, a headache on one side of the head, a stiff neck, upset stomach, hemorrhoids, ingrown toenails, all the maladies that we inherited from that devilish man, the little civil servant in the pinstriped suit, laid out to be mourned, waked, vilified, and eulogized this day from which I guess he is to be expelled from our consciousness out into the eternal vastness of the universe.

Joe sings "You Can't Always Get What You Want" along with the radio, which blasts from the speakers as we speed, windows up and air conditioner on, over the causeway, back into Clearwater, and on to the chapel. As soon as we pull into the Rhodes Funeral Parlor parking lot, the fun ends. We get serious.

"Wipe that grin off your face," I say to Joe, trying to make myself sound like our father. "Or I'll wipe it off for you."

"Okay, Chief," Joe says, sounding just like the old man.

"Hey, this is serious," Tom warns us.

"Screw you," Brendan tells him.

Then, straightening our ties, buttoning our jackets, polishing our shoes on the bottoms of our pants, we enter the funeral parlor.

I thought that the Chief would be put away already, that I wouldn't have to see him ever again, but there he is, front and center, surrounded by the horseshoe rings of flowers and well-wishings—on one of the floral wreaths it says: To Jimmy, from Your Godfather—still vigilant and scrutinizing his sons and daughters. I get hot and clammy; I don't like this Florida weather at all. Heat always brings out my dengue fever, causing me to get headaches and feel vaguely hallucinatory, like some second-rate Joseph Conrad character. Clearly I have not traveled through the five stages of grief I learned about when I had to mourn the loss of my alcohol at Smithers Alcohol and Treatment Center on East Ninety-third Street off Madison Avenue in Manhattan; I need to go through these stages in order to be well myself, though for the life of me, other than denial and anger, I can't remember what the five stages are. Oh, yes, I think, acceptance too, so I have three stages of grief at hand, fumbling to remember the others, as though that act of remembering will be a kind of substitute for actually feeling them.

I cannot kneel in front of the coffin yet again, but maybe, I think, I will be able to say a prayer from this perch in the back of the room. It would be my own kind of prayer, not denominational, not religious, but a practical utterance to God concerning my father. Yet what I say has no words only a vague feeling, and I ask myself, *If there are no words, can it be a prayer?* I think not. Maybe a meditation, yes, but not a prayer; prayers need words, and not only words, you need to believe what you are saying. I don't believe a thing I am saying. Besides, I'm not saying anything at all.

After the abortive prayer, I saunter to the back of the room again as relatives enter, sobbing and veiled, no longer talking away; now they whisper. Even amid sheer chaos, a kind of order obtains. There are rules. If I don't know the rules or don't seem to understand them, these mourners do. I sit on the sofa in the back of the chapel, the younger children playing around me. I try to put together a thumbnail portrait of my father: he became an orphan when his own father became incapable of raising him, forever drunk and in trouble, so that my father lived for a time with his late mother's relatives from New Jersey. Eventually he left New York for Washington, where he briefly attended Georgetown University, which he hoped would be his entry into the foreign service.

During his Washington years, he lived in a boarding house. The happiest stories I ever heard him tell were about those days, and when he said those words *boarding house,* they rolled off his tongue like poetry, part James Joyce short story, part Sean O'Casey play. When he talked about the boarding-house days in Washington, I pictured a house with wooden stairs on the exterior of the building, almost as if it were New Orleans, not Washington. But his boarding-house days came to a close when his father became ill, and he had to leave college and his job in Washington and come back to the city to watch after his sickly old man.

It was after he returned to Brooklyn that he met my mother, introduced to her by his best friend, the man who married my mother's sister Harriet. After he met my mother, they got married, he went off to war, and she raised their children in Greenbelt, Maryland. He got stationed once again in his beloved Washington, no longer a single, boarding-house dweller but a married sailor in Naval intelligence, his assignment the processing of west coast Japanese into the internment camps in America during World War II. By war's end, he had three sons and soon enough a daughter on the way, and by the time they moved to Long Island, getting out of Brooklyn, there were five children. They had double-digit children by the end of the fifties, though nine would remain the magic number, the number of children that was most often used when people asked him how many children he had.

"Nine," he said, using all the fingers on his two hands minus the left thumb.

Like Charlie Chan who referred to his sons as "number one" or "number two" son, my father employed a similar lexicon. I was the third son. When he wanted to put a Brooklyn spin on it, he said, "He's tray," meaning three in Italian, or "t'ree" in the more vernacular speech of East New York.

Seeing my father again is almost like seeing him yesterday. I get nervous and afraid, tight in the throat, worried, and unsure. And, like yesterday, looking at his placid face now, I remember how animated and antagonistic it used to be. When I was a teenager—the last time I was in his thrall—I hated my father; gradually I mended this emotion to angry spite and vicious innuendo. Finally, I realized that I was so angry at him because he awarded me the booby prize in the Catholic sweepstakes: being born. Everything else is gravy. His rotten personality. His evil disposition. His murderous tempers. I can forgive him all that, but I still have this grudge against him for allowing me to be born, not into infinite grace, what I yearned for, but into the misery of this Catholic childhood, its guilts and shames, its sins, both venal and mortal, and its everlasting punishments for the damned. I also used to think that if God were this mean, He probably would change the rules anytime He liked, so that instead of the good being saved and the bad condemned forever to Hell, God might condemn the good to eternal torture and admit the bad boys and girls into the pleasures of eternal life in Heaven ever after.

That is what I experience standing in the back of the chapel, hanging back, as I look up front at my shriveled father in his coffin. Maybe all their Catholic rules would not work, I think. Still, I go forward, kneel at the casket, and finally say a prayer for him, not some "Our Father/Hail Mary/Act of Contrition" kind of prayer but one of my own intensity.

"I forgive you, Dad," I say, "so I hope you forgive me. Let's be friends now. I hope you didn't suffer too much and hope you had a moment of peace before the end. If there is an afterlife, I don't want you to burn forever in Hell. You were a son of a bitch, yes, but not a totally evil man—not even a little evil, for that matter—just another working-class stiff, a shanty clown really, and I'll forever be grateful to your bequeathing each of us a sublime sense of the absurd. Take care and be well. See you around. Amen."

10

The Meeting

My oldest brother is a garrulous raconteur, someone who loves to talk, tell stories, and listen to others tell their tales. Yet Jimmy is strangely quiet. At this moment, when the casket is about to be closed and some remarks are in order, he is the one, being the oldest, expected to make those final remarks. Yet he is overwhelmed by grief. Someone must say something though. Instead of Jimmy, Peter stands and speaks in a muted, consoling voice that I hadn't heard him use with anyone since we were boys. Not that Peter can't be consoling, understanding, and bright; that is probably his first nature.

"Let's close with the Saint Francis prayer," he says, after instructing everyone about the itinerary to the church and then to the cemetery.

His new teeth did not arrive in time, so he delivers the eulogy in this gummy toothless way, kind of like Gabby Hayes. That's who he looks like, not this renegade from New York, but some old prospector, bearded, grizzled, in dungarees and cowboy boots and a green sportscoat several sizes too small for him. I can't hear a word he says, mainly because the sight of him behind the podium transfixes me; I am more interested in the man than the message—forget the medium—and, besides, what can he say about our father that I don't already know or feel? None of us would tolerate Peter if he got sappy and corny and said things that none of us believed. So he keeps it simple.

An usher closes the lid on the coffin.

The American flag that was draped over the coffin is folded. Everyone must assemble outside, we are told. No one but the six brothers remains to carry the casket. A cortege assembles. We are to make our way slowly around the corner to the church. The six of us line up, three on each side, to carry the coffin to the hearse, and then, once it is in place in the hearse, to go around the corner to Saint Cecilia's and the funeral Mass. The oak box seems to weigh hundreds of pounds. I want to laugh and cry at the same time. Instead, I sweat under the strain of lifting and then carrying the coffin.

As we move slowly toward the door with the coffin in our hands, I remember that my mother, the night before, decided that Joe most closely approximated his father's physical size, and so, rather than cremate the old man in the nice pin-striped suit he wore, they'd remove it, and Joe would become the beneficiary of this parental largesse. But like everything else in the family, there is a story connected to the suit. Years ago, when Kaitlin was still married to the clothing executive who was her first husband and Dustin's father, and during their marriage, when they lived in New Hampshire and then Connecticut, he was in charge of the Ralph Lauren Polo factory in New England. He got my father to come for a visit to New Hampshire and then had one of the Polo tailors fashion the pin-striped suit for him. But it didn't take a genius to know that my father would never wear a thousand-dollar suit anywhere while he was alive. All along, it had become the suit he'd be buried in. Now Joe would get the suit.

Carrying him from the chapel to the hearse outside is a chore, even with the six of us strong, if not in shape. Jimmy complains that he may have thrown out his shoulder. Peter whistles and says how heavy the old boy is. Joe, Tommy, and Brendan carry the casket silently while I just sweat and worry that the heat and humidity and now this exertion are going to trigger a bout of the tropical disease. But we all hold on, finally reaching the hearse, the back door of the black Cadillac open, and we place the casket onto the rollers built into the floor, and the gigantic box with the shriveled little Irishman inside—wearing his fancy suit for the last time before they cremate him—goes effortlessly forward into the hearse.

I walk across the parking lot to the church and wait there for the others. Once again we have to lift the casket collectively and then march, slow-motion, into the church for the funeral Mass. Once everyone is seated, the six of us brothers march with the heavy oak box, ever so slowly, forward to the front altar. We dislodge the casket onto a stand. Then we each file into a pew reserved for us. By now I am sweating so much I wonder if any liquid remains in my body, and I wish that I had drunk more water.

The Mass proceeds until that point when the Franciscan priest delivers the eulogy.

"He was a sweet, quiet, gentle, kind, peaceful, little man," the priest says at one point.

I think it is that perennial clown Joe who whispers— though a little too loudly—to the rest of us, "Who the fuck is he talking about?"

"Sssshhhh," goes one of my sisters in the pew in front of us, which nearly puts me into conniptions, and for the rest of the service I have to restrain myself, not from crying, as everyone thinks I am on the verge of doing, but laughing riotously.

The priest drones on, removing the old man, the Chief, from our midst, and providing the public with a man named James Stephens, someone whom none of us knows. No one who knew my father ever called him James Stephens except maybe a bill collector. This James Stephens sounds like nearly every other retired, Catholic, male civil servant in Clearwater. "He was hardworking, honest, quiet, sincere, courageous, a good father," the priest drones on, "a dearly beloved spouse, a member of Catholic organizations, particularly in James Stephens's case, the Knights of Columbus, and he was a local parishioner, a regular at the eleven o'clock Mass on Sunday." No matter that he never spoke to anyone and quickly bolted across the way for the coffee and donuts once the service ended.

The only person comforted by this routine is my mother, the one for whom it is intended. It is as if she and the priest have a conspiracy to obscure who the old man was. He certainly was never a quiet, sweet, gentle, kind, peaceful man, or whatever it was that the priest just uttered moments earlier. There was a bit of the savage in my father, and it was the part of him I liked the best, and the part, I think, that pleased his daughters and other sons too.

He was stubborn, willful, bellicose, tendentious, and sometimes small minded. Earlier, Jimmy, while we waited at the chapel to go to the Mass, repeated our father's philosophy once again, "All dames are wacky. That includes your dear mother." *Wacky* was his favorite word to describe a lot of things. Wacky dames. Wacky kids. Wacky neighbors. Wacky priests. Wacky palm trees. Wacky alligators. Wacky cars. Wacky clothes. Wacky music. Wacky food. Wacky furniture. Why doesn't the priest mention that? Simply using the word *wacky* would get a laugh out of everyone. Besides, they at least would recognize the man whose requiem this is supposed to be.

I look at my brothers' and sisters' faces and I see that they agree with me—our father is missing from the eulogy. The man who takes his place, this James Stephens, is present for our mother, who needs this fellow, for whatever reasons, to put a closure to the life of her former husband. After all, living or dead, we are simply this man's children, though our mother has just gone from loving wife to widow. Being a widow takes some getting used to, and I think maybe that mourning James Stephens instead of the old man or the Chief or Stevie or Stewart or Jimmy is a way for our mother to become a widow and no longer be a wife.

We sit there and absorb the words, listen to the music from the choir loft—a woman soloist accompanied by an organ, singing "Amazing Grace" and "Ave Maria"—and then file out, numbly, sweating and a little shaky. One day some Franciscan will be up there intoning about what a good, gentle, kind, peaceful, loving, caring, wonderful man Michael Stephens was, though I have not been inside a church for most of my adult life, and even if I might aspire to some of those conditions, I rarely, if ever, inhabit them with any certainty. Like my father, I am edgy, temperamental, judgmental, and, on occasion, explosive and dangerous. So are my sisters and brothers. Wouldn't anyone remember those facts when we were gone, that try as we might, we were not always very nice people? What would the minister say about my brothers and sisters? Let the priest say we were ruthlessly honest, that we wouldn't let the wool stay over our eyes, that our ideals were impossible; just let them say that, though I know no priest ever would. It was not in a priest to be so honest about a mortal; we had to fit some stereotype that he had learned about at the seminary.

The limousines assemble in front of the funeral parlor. Then the cortege winds out of Clearwater toward the veterans' cemetery in Saint Petersburg. Yet my father won't be buried today; they first have to cremate, and then on another day, the family who live here will assemble for a smaller service at which the ashes will be interred in the ground. Brendan asks the driver of our limo to crank up some rock 'n' roll, which he does; the car's stereo is superb, reminding me that, besides funerals, these rented limos are often used to deflower virgins at senior proms and to transport drunken groomsmen and bridesmaids to motels for quick trysts after the wedding. This knowledge is comforting because it tells me that, no matter what, the world keeps grinding on. In fact, because he was not some kind of senior officer in the Navy but only a chief petty officer, the family has been asked, after this simple send-off, to wait until after Veterans Day, a few weeks away, for the official burial of the remains.

I suck on a bottle of Poland Spring water, both the bottle

and I sweating. My temples pulse and pound, and I have a migraine headache, so I take some ibuprofen to relieve the pressure on the right side of my head. I have a slight shake in my hands, something I've noticed often now that I am sober and able to notice such things. I am a nervous person, though maybe everyone in the family is pent up and nervous. I want to ask Brendan or Tommy for a cigarette, but I hold back, not wishing to start that nasty habit all over again. I look out the window at the drab neon landscape of the local highway. McDonald's, Checkers, KFC, Wendy's, Arby's, Burger King, Roy Rogers, Long John Silver, and Treacher's flash by the smoky tinted windows. Even though it is the middle of a weekday, the traffic is thick, even clotted, and it takes some time to get to the cemetery. When I look up ahead, I see the hearse and the other limos with the rest of the family in them, and behind us, I see my sister Peggy, her husband, and her daughter in their van. Peggy's face is puffy and swollen, with streaks of makeup running down her cheeks.

The cars roll up to the entrance of the cemetery where we stop to get clearance to proceed. Once cleared, we drive to the memorial site. When I get out of the limo, I experience the heat and humidity again, and after removing the coffin from the hearse, we carry it to a stone table and put it down. The six sons have to face the other mourners. I see my mother's face, how forlorn and upset she looks. No longer jolly old Rosie, she has become this vulnerable little lady in her late seventies, her eyes full of tears, her husband gone forever, and her own life filled with grief and recognition, first for this newly passed husband and then for her own life. It is the first time that I look at my own mother without seeing the fresh-faced young Catholic schoolgirl. The tears roll down her cheeks, and she looks so tiny.

A potbellied soldier from the local American Legion hall delivers the eulogy. He is a friend of my father, and a man, at least in his physique, who bears a resemblance to my father before the strokes and the dementia; it is reassuring to see him, even if his words, read from a generic text, are even less personal than the priest's were. At least the style and tone are right. A twenty-one-gun salute is fired from old M-1 rifles, the air cracking with the gunfire. Then a piper plays, though terribly off-key, a version of "Danny Boy." Even though the pipes are out of tune and the man lacks for a certain grace and musicianship, nonetheless the pipes create the desired effect. I find myself crying behind my dark glasses, and I notice everyone else crying too. Before this moment, I never understood how good—how cleansing, how purifying—grieving is. At last, we are mourning, we have mourned the dead, and he is dead. He is gone, and we cry for him.

The coffin is lifted into the hearse and the black wagon drives off, back toward the traffic of the highway and Clearwater where my father, minus his suit that will go to Joe, is to be turned into a pile of ashes. Almost like seeing a movie, I watch the hearse slowly drive down the long tree-lined roadway in the cemetery, and soon it disappears—and he is gone forever. More aimless chatting and condolences take place, and then we regroup and get back into the limos, this time to go to another favorite restaurant of my parents, one of those places that caters to older white people's bland tastes in food.

The maître d' puts us in a room off the main one and quickly it fills up with about twenty people: brothers and sisters, their children, spouses.

After ordering the food, the noise escalates, only this time the whir is not like it had been in the previous restaurant or at the funeral parlor. This is a release, a letting go.

Some of the older nieces and nephews drink wine while the nondrinking relatives gape at them in wonder and alarm. I know that my siblings are asking themselves, just as I am, if this is the next generation to be abused by alcohol. We are a nice enough family in the absence of booze, but with it in us, we become unpredictable, even treacherous, to ourselves and the surroundings and the people in our social orbit. More important than moralizing about booze, I have a visceral reaction to their drinking. Watching my nieces and nephews drink triggers the compulsion in me. This is not a moral issue but a physical one. It is also a mental and spiritual problem I am facing. I want what I want when I want it. Those words rush through me like a song by James Brown. I want what I want when I want it. What I want is a drink and when I want it is now. I want to join my nieces and nephews. I want to get drunk. For, after all, isn't that what one is supposed to do at an Irish wake? You are supposed to bury the dead, then get trashed on alcohol. Even people who don't drink get drunk at Irish wakes. Why can't I?

But I can't. Nor can most of my siblings. The concern I have for my nieces and nephews is paralleled by another feeling: envy. I am jealous that they are drinking and I am not.

I pull Joe aside and ask, "You want to go to a meeting?"

"A meeting?" he asks. Then he says. "Oh, you mean a meeting."

"Yeah," I say, "a meeting."

"Why didn't you say so," says Joe, and he gets a few others to go with us after Jimmy explains to him how to get to the clubhouse meeting nearby.

A bunch of us climb aboard the white rental van and head out for a little medicine. We park in a lot next to the clubhouse, a run-down building in a dicey part of town. We walk into a room already filled up with people waiting for a meeting too. We sit down, look around, make ourselves at home.

The chairperson asks if there are any visitors; I don't want to raise my hand and say I am from New York, figuring it would get me in trouble in a place like this, fellowship or no fellowship. But Tommy, unable to contain himself, raises his hand and tells everyone that the five of us are from New York and are down in Florida for our father's funeral, blah blah blah. The first guy to share says that he knows it's a fellowship and all, but he'll be glad when "all these fucking New Yorkers get out of town," he says, "and take a Canadian under each arm when you go."

The Toronto Blue Jays, a foreign enterprise that stole the national symbol of the World Series from the United States, has its training camp here.

I want to stand up and punch this guy in the nose because I am in no mood to be insulted by a dumbbell cracker redneck asshole from Florida. I guess my kid brother Brendan feels the same way. I merely have evil thoughts toward this alcoholic. Brendan has words ready for him.

My brother stands, shakes a threatening fist in the man's direction, and says, "I don't need your bullshit. You hear me? And if you don't like what I'm saying, we can settle this outside. We'll forget about the meeting and the words and everything. We'll forget this is a fellowship, and we'll settle it the old way, outside, me and you, okay, wise guy?"

Brendan would just as soon take it outside and settle it with a couple of hard body shots and hooks, crosses and uppercuts to the head.

I probably never loved my kid brother more than I did at that moment of solidarity with him.

Less a fellowship meeting, it feels like a night on the town in some shit-kicker bar. It is almost as if the air has been sucked out of the room. One by one, people raise their hands and, in this way of solidarity, let the local toughs know that they, too, are New Yorkers visiting Florida, convincing the homeboys that it isn't worth engaging the grieving brothers because these other New Yorkers will join in the fracas. I don't know how we do it, but we get through the entire meeting without an incident beyond the initial confrontation, and upon leaving, though no one comes up to us to say hello or good-bye, we get out of there alive and in one piece. The Stephenses, 1; The Clubhouse Regulars, 0.

After the meeting, no one wants to go back to the motel, even though we have to catch a flight the next day to New

York. And no one wants to go back to my mother's place, the rooms too small and too many relatives staying there. Instead, we drive north to Jimmy's new place, an hour's drive away.

Jimmy jumped through more hoops and accomplished more transformations than anyone else in the family. Once a wino working out of the local caddy yard in East Williston, a periodic visitor to nuthouses with the regularity of a Seiko watch, and a frequent habitué of the local precinct house, Jimmy was the second—after our mother—to get sober in the family, and though not the first, he became the foremost advocate of sobriety, his new high and religion. He and my mother started out in Williston Park and were, by the time the family moved to Florida, old-timers in Albertson and other working-class towns on Long Island. When my parents moved south, Jimmy soon followed, and although my mother stopped going to meetings, he doubled up his efforts, so that years later, Jimmy once again was a legendary old-timer down in Florida too. He is far removed from being a caddy-shack wino; now he is a husband and father, and his son is a reincarnation of our father—in his looks, the gestures, the way he eyeballs you like a tough guy, but mostly in his spirit, the absurd energy and the ridiculously serious manners that turn instantly comic.

Once we get to Jimmy's house north of Clearwater, though, we each realize how tired we are. We say hello, then good-bye, and within fifteen minutes, we go back to the motel, even though we drove almost an hour to get to his house. We have to return the van and get to the airport by noon, and I want to find an early morning meeting so that I won't leave Florida with a bad taste from the guy who wanted us to leave town. Today, I think, I no longer have a father.

Once again, lights out, resting in bed at the Blue Jay Motel, I think back on the day. A long time ago, I used to picture this moment I inhabit now, and I would think of how concerned I would be about my father's funeral; I would reflect on the funeral Mass and the cemetery rituals or on my father's life. But I keep seeing my nieces and nephews drinking at the restaurant afterward. The urge I got watching them drink was enormous, one of the biggest ones I have ever had. It reminds me now to be grateful because I did not drink in spite of that enormous feeling to do so. I often have heard it said that at some point every alcoholic in recovery will be face-to-face with a drink. Meetings, friends, Steps, the fellowship—nothing will help facing down this one drink. The only thing that will keep me sober is a Higher Power. That is the only thing big enough to fit between me and that enormous drink begging to be drunk by no one else but me. It has my name written on it. I can taste it too. It is cool and refreshing; sinister, yes; cunning, powerful, oh yes; but most of all, it beckons me. And I can't resist.

My nieces and nephews are terrifically handsome kids. They are good-looking and energetic, alive and well. But what I remember about them is their drinking. Not that they were drunk. Because they were not. They simply were drinking. That is an innocuous enough activity if your name is not Stephens. But their name is Stephens. So I find myself thinking about that relationship between my family and drinking. Alcohol is a kind of jet fuel to my family. Occasionally, though, I wish, despite that fact, that I could drown my own feelings in a tub of beer and a jug of whiskey, maybe even do a few lines, not of coke but of something down and dirty like heroin, and then top it off with a bunch of pills, just like in the old days, and then slowly watch this movie disappear into a gray haze of unreality, *slow fade*, through each moment as it turned weird; I would think to myself that now I have arrived at the ultimate reality, this numb pain cauterized by drugs and alcohol, the pain vanishing and the numbness coming to the fore until there is nothing left but numbness, and I would lie to myself saying that I have arrived at the ultimate truth and how honest and fresh it is to discover this fact, that alcohol and drugs liberate the senses, bring one so close to the edge of knowing, that booze and pills reveal the greater reality behind the veil, although I might think this thought for only a millisecond, and then it would vanish into the haze, and I would find myself lurching from one truth to the next the way I once lurched from barstools in a dingy saloon at the edge of town, and somewhere around midnight it would all explode in a fury of violence, us against the rednecks, the rednecks against the white boys from up north, and maybe that is how my father wanted to be remembered and how we should pay him homage, but I decided to opt out of that scenario, so that instead of doing that, instead of drinking with the nieces and nephews, I had a glass of club soda and ate a fish dinner, and afterward a bunch of us went off to a meeting in Clearwater.

The only thing between me and a drink this afternoon was God. So I thank Him or Her or It. *You got me through another one,* I pray. So thank You.

11

Farewell to the Chief

I wake early, around six in the morning, take the van, and drive over the causeway into Clearwater. I go up the steps of a church and into a back room where a bunch of people are having a meeting. I introduce myself by my first name, explain why I am here, and become one of them. The whole concept, so simple it is almost ridiculous, is also profound and, if I say so myself, tailor-made for the Stephens family. On this morning, the day after his funeral, I do not believe my father died of natural causes. (The members of my family have yet to determine what really kills us.) Rather, I see my father's death as another manifestation of the disease that has killed my family on both sides and that prompted my attendance at the meeting—alcoholism.

Technically speaking, my father died from heart failure. It was compounded by his dementia, which in turn was the result of many strokes, some small, some large, all of them clustered into the last couple of years of his life. I think my brother Peter hit it on the head the night before when he said that the old man had gone weird on us after his prostate operation. Peter went on to say that the Chief had lied to the anesthesiologist. When asked if he was a big drinker, he hedged and said that he was not.

I remember one of those medical lectures we received when I was a patient at Smithers Alcohol and Treatment

Center in New York about how alcoholics react differently to ether because it's a chemical whose molecular structure bears a resemblance to alcohol's. Because alcoholics metabolize alcohol differently than nonalcoholics do—which, finally, is all that an alcoholic is, a person with an allergy to booze—they react differently to ether. I remember the Irish nurse at Smithers telling us that, working in operating rooms, she knew when she had an alcoholic on her hands because he or she would wake up in the middle of an operation. Why? Because alcoholics need more anesthesia than nonalcoholics; they need enough to convince their bodies that the anesthesia is not ethyl alcohol, its friend and demon, its being and its all, the body's nemesis, its dark other.

So my father lied. He told the doctor that he was a moderate drinker, though even a casual look at the man would tell you that he was lying. He was a boozer from way back, probably from when he was a young boy in East New York, Brooklyn, a street kid and a wise guy trying to impress the adults and prove to them that he was a big shot. Alcohol and big-shotism go hand in hand, and big shots are bad patients invariably because they do not cooperate; they are not willing to bend. They are rigid and they fight, as my father did all the way—from the deepening circles of the anesthesia's blur right up to the moment he bolted awake, screaming like a scared wild animal. So my father did not fare well during the operation, which was not for cancer—that would come later when he was deep into his dementia—but for a prostate problem. It was a minor operation with major results, because my father came out of it a different man—he suffered a serious stroke in the midst of the surgery. That is Peter's theory, at least, and it is, I think, a reasonable one. It confirms my thought that our family cannot know what kills us naturally. My grandfathers, my uncles, various aunts have died from boozing directly or indirectly, one way or the other.

That is another revelation I came upon here in Clearwater. I never knew that my father had been sober himself for—depending upon who told you—anywhere from five to seven years, from around the time when he approached retirement as a boss at Kennedy Airport to that moment when he and my mother sold the house on Long Island and retired to Florida. Sometime, either before moving or after arriving in Clearwater, he went back to drinking, and, as anyone with a drinking problem will tell you, it never gets better once you go back to drinking; as is so often the case, it got a lot worse.

Oh, it was fine on the surface. My father had a good life down there: no children, no mortgages, no responsibilities, only horseshoes and snooker, shuffleboard and casual walks, dinners for two and movies, and long-distance calls to relatives back in New York who seemed to be a million miles away. But when you don't drink for five years and then go back to it, the results are disastrous. Alcoholism is called a progressive disease because each time a drinker with this illness drinks, it gets worse and worse. Even if he hadn't had a drink for five years, once my father went back to the booze, it was as if he had been drinking all those years—his body craved the stuff even more. Slowly but surely, my father was killing himself, doing it by way of our family's poison of choice, something his father knew about, and his stepmother, his stepsister, and his half-sisters, all of whom had a similar jones, or addiction, for hooch.

If my mother, brothers, sisters, and I do not drink, we will find out what will kill us in the end. Who knows—maybe we will die earlier if we don't drink. But that is something I am willing to find out. In fact, I would prefer a shorter life to the hell that longtime drinkers descend into, dementia being but one of the places where alcohol takes us. I sit in this room in the back of a church in downtown Clearwater, the sun not quite up, and I listen to these people talking, and I am glad—relieved—to be among them.

After the meeting, I go back to the Blue Jay Motel to wake my brothers and prepare for our return to New York. We have a long day, and I notice that Tommy is getting more difficult. He asked my mother if he could stay on in her apartment, but she wouldn't let him. She told him that if he managed to stay sober for six months, she'd have him down in the spring. Now he is unclear about whether the rehab he was in will let him back, because, though he had a legitimate reason, he left without permission. Over the past five days, the three of us—Brendan, Joe, and I—have gotten into this locker-room kind of humor, and the Polish couple who became the Pronskys are at the center of this. I knew that at some point Tom was going to call this couple who ran the motel the Pronskys, and, apparently, he already had. Neither of them seemed to know what the hell he was talking about. Fortunately, his saying the wrong name was combined with the mountain of words that perpetually rolled off his tongue. The couple did not notice. Poor Tom.

We wait outside by the white van wondering when Tom would be ready. Every couple of minutes he sticks his head out his window and gives us a status report on his packing. This strikes me as peculiar because he has hardly anything with him but the clothes on his back. Still, he is too disorganized to get himself out of the room and into the van. We are to go back to our mother's to say good-bye, then to the airport where we will return the van and hop on our plane for New York. Although it disturbed me a few days earlier how physical everyone was with Tom—hitting him on the arm, slapping him on the head, not terribly hard but still enough for me to notice—I now find myself thinking violent thoughts about him, and not for the first time this trip. What is his problem? Why doesn't he get ready and down to the van? I had awakened him more than two hours ago. But it is no use trying to reason with him. Tom has a problem, a deep-seated one, a real disorder, so it is better not to explode, which only would make him more nervous.

When he does come outside, chatting away to the "Pronskys," he seems indifferent to the fact that we have been waiting by the van for more than a half hour. Brendan gives him a noogie on the head. Joe shoves him into the van. Right away he takes up his endless monologue about nothing and everything, the moon and stars, dogs on the prowl, birds in the bayou, the price of a new guitar—all of it disjointed, virtually nonstop non sequiturs. We decide to eat breakfast at an upscale diner at the entrance to the beach, a diner with ersatz fifties decor, including murals of

The Honeymooners, I Love Lucy characters, *Your Show of Shows,* Jack Benny, and Milton Berle. After ordering food for a small army, Tom immediately hits on the waitresses, telling them about himself, his brothers, his family, his father's funeral—anything and everything that comes into his mind and out of his mouth simultaneously. And then Brendan and Tom are at each other because Tom feels that his baby brother doesn't respect him enough.

"Why should I respect you?" Brendan asks.

"Because I'm your older brother," Tom says, his logic flawless as he sings out this refrain of our entire trip. "I'm your older brother."

"You're a bum," answers Brendan, matter-of-factly.

"Now you sound like the Chief."

"Hey, get a job; quit mooching off me."

"Speaking of which," Tom says, "I need you to cover me for breakfast, loan me a few bucks for cigarettes and also a little extra to hold me over when I get back to the rehab on the Island."

"What Brendan's saying, Tom," Joe interrupts, "is that you can't keep expecting him to bail you out all the time."

"Hey, quit ganging up on me, all right?" Tom demands, getting defensive.

His defensiveness reminds me, in an exaggerated way, of my own way of dealing with adversity. I make a note of it. I think my defensiveness cost me my last three or four jobs. It is probably why I have been unemployed for much of the past two years and why I am verging on being unemployable. All my family's problems are the very same problems that plague me. I have a short temper like Brendan said he has at work. I become defensive, "get into your fight-or-flight mode," as my wife calls it, when challenged or criticized. In fact, I can't take criticism, and it makes me wonder how I endured—or was endured—in two graduate programs: one for writing, the other for drama. Like Joe, I am an isolator; I want most to crawl into my domestic cocoon and say good-bye to the rest of the world, making a separate peace and going my merry way. Like my brother Jimmy, there are times when I become manic and other times when I am depressed for months on end. Like my brother Peter, toothless and riddled with insult and injury, I catalog the long list of my resentments and vow to get revenge on everyone who ignores or persecutes me. Like my mother and sisters, I think that I can finesse my way through everything, that a little charm, a little upbeat spin, a trace of a dimpled smile, will solve everything, but it will not. Like my father was, I am a rager, a railer, a fist-shaker, a man who digs in his heels when threatened, a little bull-terrier—the kind that locks its jaws onto someone or something and never lets go—a man full of invective, spleen, gall, bile, sputum, mucous, and treacly sentimentality that I foist off as honest and sincere feeling.

What I mean to say is that I am no different than any of these family members, least of all poor Tommy, that hopeless, homeless vagrant, that endless talker and explainer and defender, that edgy, uncomfortable, ill-at-ease presence at the end of the table, who spills his coffee twice, tips over Joe's orange juice, knocks over Brendan's water, and lectures me that I curse too much, that I take the name of the Lord in vain, that I am an idolater, a heathen, and a nonbeliever.

"Screw you and eat your cinnamon pancakes, Tommy," I say. Even if we are alike, I still don't have to listen to his grief. "Screw you and shut up."

"You'd think because Mike was a writer that he could talk better than a truck driver," Tom says.

"You got a problem with truck drivers?" Brendan, a truck driver himself, asks.

"No, no, no," Tom says nervously, "I'm just saying . . ."

"What are you saying?" Joe asks.

"Hey!" Tom shouts. "Look! Above you! It's Jackie Gleason!"

Then he is off on another one of his monologues that go nowhere. He talks about Jackie Gleason, bowling, running shoes, the Beatles; he asks another dumb question about my writing, another dumb question about Joe's new house; he criticizes Brendan's attitude and comments on the waitresses' legs. All of this is delivered in one breathless sentence—without pause or facile rhythm—that rushes out of him like foul air. Poor Tom.

On the drive into Clearwater, we blast the stereo system in the van, rocking and rolling our father into eternity. Once again Tom takes umbrage; he doesn't like the way the three of us behave in the immediate aftermath of our father's end. He would be right, of course, if we were people other than the people we are. Even in traditional Irish funerals it is considered proper to misbehave afterward. That is what a wake is for, to act out and carry on, and since none of us drinks anymore, at least we can carry on in the van, telling Michael Jackson jokes.

"That's enough," Tom shouts, "I've heard enough of this!"

"Shut up," Joe says, matter-of-factly, even kindly, and keeps driving.

At my mother's, Peter and his children are awake but still eating breakfast. When I was a child, I remembered that though my mother was not a housekeeper of any rank—our house was filthy and disorganized—she made meals for people all day long. Now she is back to her old routines, and I can't tell whether she likes it or not. It has been so many years since this many people wanting to be fed and sheltered have been in her house.

Peter's children are the oldest of the grandchildren; in some respects they are my mother's favorites. When someone tells Peter's son Brendan that he looks a little bit like Tom Cruise—and he does—my mother adds, "Oh, Brendan's handsomer than Tom Cruise." Once my mother said that Tom Cruise looked like me too, I recall, and then I realize that Tom Cruise is probably her favorite actor because he looks, at certain angles and moments, like everyone in the family, including my mother herself, Mrs. Cruise.

Tom—my brother, not the actor—leaves the three brothers he has been running with for the past five days and lingers around his nieces and nephews and his sister Rosemary, who is there with her two large, sleek greyhounds.

Coffee is brewed. Coffee cake is eaten. Cigarettes are smoked. But mostly pot after pot of coffee is drunk. Nowadays the coffeepot has replaced the beer bottle, and it is ubiquitous. Everyone drinks coffee, and after one pot is made, another is quickly started. The room smells of coffee and cigarettes, coffee cake and people.

Better to leave Florida without resentment, mourning my father but thankful that he didn't have to suffer any longer with his dementia and the terrors of that ailment. At least he could find some peace in the eternal moment, whatever it is and wherever he might be, whatever form he might manifest himself into—spirit or simply new molecules, wave action in the sea, a worm in the ground, a ray of sunlight from the sky, a dog on a leash, a million-year-old rock, a bicycle, a lollipop, an auto part, a strand of wild-assed DNA, a whisper across the wind. We came to my mother's place to say good-bye to her and the other members of the family. Joe collects our father's suits, Tommy annoys other family members, Brendan talks with his nieces and nephews, and I call New York to say I'll be there later in the day.

My mother sits at the dining-room table talking with her grandchildren from North Carolina and Texas, and it suddenly occurs to me that it is she, not my father, who is the real talker in the family. Maybe I don't mean talker, because it was hard to top my father for sheer talk. My mother—although I didn't realize it until just now—is the storyteller in the family. Years ago, I would have said that my father or oldest brother or my Irish stepgrandmother was the storyteller. The style of speaking that my mother employs is so low-key and self-effacing that it is hard to realize how artful some of her tales are. These other relatives, I realize, are talkers, not storytellers, purveyors of news, not legends. Everything my mother says is a set piece. She has been telling us stories since we were children, and each retelling is simply a variation on the theme.

What also obscures her storytelling gift is that no one

associates words with my mother. Instead, they think of babies. I spent my childhood seeing her perpetually swollen belly and her seasonal trips back to Saint Mary's hospital in Bedford-Stuyvesant, Brooklyn. My mother was the Henry Ford of maternity, the cloning machine, a human Galapagos turtle who, no matter where she was on Long Island, had to come back to the ancestral soil to give birth. Brooklyn was an ontological place, good for birthing and burying.

Every story my mother ever told was set in Brooklyn— not a borough in turmoil but an idyllic place. There were no ghettos or crime; this was a gaslit world of brownstones, trolleys, horse-drawn carts, iceboxes, coal cellars. Most important, it was a world fueled by social and moral order. My mother never spoke of neighborhoods in these sagas, but of parishes: Our Lady of Lourdes, Saint John's, and Saint Gregory's. Everyone was Irish—or at least Catholic— in my mother's Brooklyn, but unlike the potato-picking bog men of my father's immigrant clan, these were old-time New Yorkers, who may have once lived in Albany and Manhattan but had married into families from the eastern borough so long ago that their previous lives outside the territory were only hearsay. Her relatives were merchants and newspapermen, lawyers and builders.

By contrast, we, her children, grew up ghettoized, either in East New York or in the working-class suburbs of Long Island. In a crowded little house filled with nine children, not to mention an occasional grandparent or a miscreant uncle sleeping off a drunk on the couch, her stories were told in the dining room over table wine and Salem cigarettes, and, thinking about her now, she appeared as exotic then as Scheherazade, and Brooklyn was the setting of her Arabian nights.

My mother's Brooklyn does not exist anymore and may never have existed except in her mind. Yet I have gone to Bedford-Stuyvesant and seen the house she was born and grew up in. In its heyday, it had twenty-six rooms, and several generations of her family had been born in it. Later it would become a convent, then a rooming house. Today it no longer exists, except as a vivid shelter in my mother's imagination, and in her stories.

The best stories concern losing the house. Her father was a bailbondsman and haberdasher. He had been mugged outside the Tombs and afterward lost his memory. This was followed by the Depression. In the thirties, when she was a teenager, the family lived in a succession of rundown tenements and ended up in a small apartment in Crown Heights. Misfortune, as she tells it, became her strength; adversity only made her more grateful.

Besides, she adored her family, especially her father, who was a sweet, daft old man, good-looking and extremely well-dressed, a figure from another time. He epitomized that gaslit world of her imagination and may have been its inspiration. Not long before, though, she had told me a story about her father that was not from the grand house days. It was the story of their struggles through Brooklyn and that long march of downward mobility throughout the Depression. As my mother approaches her seventy-ninth birthday, her stories are no longer so idealized. They become grittier with time and with our own circumstances.

Her father had purchased his usual supply of bootleg gin. A son transported the large bottle home. At the steps—called the stoop in Brooklyn—the son (my dear uncle Jimmy) lost his purchase on the bottle of gin, and it slipped out of his hands and broke. That swell old idyllic father in pin-striped suit, high starched collar, bow tie, and waxed mustache proceeded to beat his son unconditionally.

When I heard this, I was not so much shocked as relieved. At last her stories resembled a world I was familiar with, a world of drinking, domestic violence, and passions out of control. The backdrop was not the scrim for a musical about New York but the real thing itself. I saw tenements, stoops, and rugged streets. This was Brooklyn as I remembered it and as I would probably convey it to my own grandchildren someday. It was a Brooklyn of enormous feelings, some of them disproportionate and unreal.

All this reminds me of something that Isaac Bashevis Singer said: If feelings were money, we'd all be millionaires. When Brooklyn is mentioned, I think of my own childhood, certainly, but also the hundreds of relatives I knew from there, and then the ghosts of thousands of ancestors. But I also think of the downward mobility of my mother's tales, how her gentrified family slipped from their house into tenements and then disappeared for good. Yet, somehow, remembering this does not necessarily bring bad feelings.

No fallen southern aristocrat has anything on my mother. My mother's Brooklyn is not a world of facts but one of imaginative possibility, a voicing—a register of joy and sorrow—that forever plays in my own head like a favorite tune. All this was gone now that my father died, my mother became a widow, and most of my family lived in Florida.

I am about to return to New York, the city, my own family, my own uncertainties. I kiss my mother and other relatives good-bye, hop into the van, and head toward the airport. Leaving is anticlimactic, almost routine, and without event. Because we badger Tom so much about being late, he manages to come out of the house, and we leave more or less on time.

Once again, on the drive to the airport, Tom can't stop talking, so I offer him—a homeless, broke person—twenty dollars if he will not speak for half an hour. Within five minutes, he turns around and says, "Can I say something?"

"You spoke!"

"Just one thing and I'll be quiet."

"But that was not the deal."

Then he goes off into his stream of consciousness, rattling on about nothing and everything, his monologue, without a core, just a din of words, pouring out of him nervously and without relief. I realize that he doesn't have much choice in the matter, that he can't stop talking even if he wants to.

Within fifteen minutes, Tom and Brendan begin arguing again, this time because Tom said something negative about Brendan, even though Brendan, time and again, has helped Tom out of scrapes and predicaments and has provided food and shelter for him when everyone else, including his parents and other siblings and friends, abandoned him.

Joe drops Tom and Brendan at the airport, but as soon as Tom sees that Joe and I are going somewhere else, he balks and wants to jump back into the van. He is terrified about being left alone at the airport. We explain to him that it is for only a few minutes; we have to return the van and will come back to this very spot. And we do. The return takes no longer than fifteen minutes, and yet when we get back to the airport, Tom paces, stumbling, mumbling, chattering under his breath, looking grim and humorless, dark and battered.

It seems that there is a problem. Our flight is stuck in Fort Meyers with brake failure. The airline doesn't know when the flight will arrive, but they check us in anyway. We go upstairs for coffee and juice, and Tom goes back to antagonizing Brendan. He also begins to antagonize Joe, the only brother so far who hasn't laid into him. Now he does, telling Tom to shut the hell up and listen, to sit on his hands, button his lip, take the cotton out of his ears.

I can't capture, I realize, just what it is that Tom does to annoy everyone. Reflecting upon him, it almost seems like a subjective reading of his behavior, and yet it isn't just the family who feels this way. Nearly everyone who comes into contact with him eventually has this reaction. Partly it is his barrage of questions—not one, not even one at a time, but one after the other after the other after the other, nonstop and without end.

"How is your wife?" he asks. "And your daughter? And your apartment? Is it okay? How is your block? Why do they have those funny lights on your block? What's that stuff called on the ground? Oh, yeah, concrete. You like the new Dodges? I'm looking for a new guitar. You think I could make it as a singer if I tried? What time is it? Who has a cigarette? Did you guys like the eggs this morning? Did you like the juice we just had? Hey, is this coffee any good? It tastes funny. Did you see those shoes that Mommy was wearing? How come the wheels on the van weren't white? The van was white. How come? How come you had to return the van so far away? Where is that place? Is that Tampa or Saint Pete? Is it daylight saving time down here? I guess that doesn't count anymore. Is it afternoon already? Hey, what month is this? Is this Thursday?" (It is Wednesday.) "I wonder if they're going to throw me out of the rehab I'm staying at because I been gone almost a week. Did I tell you about the rules there? It's tough. Is that in Freeport or Hempstead? I can't remember. Roosevelt? That's right. It's Roosevelt. That's usually a black town, but in this case, the rehab has black and white people, no Asians, no Puerto Ricans. No, no, no. One Puerto Rican, one Dominican guy. Hey, Mike, do people think that your daughter is Asian or American? Do people mistake your daughter for being American?" (I tell him that she is American.) "How could she be American?" he asks. "Her mother is Korean." (I tell him that she's American because she was born in New York City.) "Oh, yeah," he says, "she was born in New York. That's right. So I guess that makes her American? But people must think that she's Asian, right? They think she's Asian, even though she's American? Am I right, Mike?"

On and on Tom goes, asking and asking but, strangely, never listening, never seeming to want a response to his endless questions.

Our flight never arrives from Fort Myers. Finally the airline suggests putting some of us on other carriers. But, for whatever reason, Joe and Tom stay behind with Brendan, who is unable to switch flights because he is traveling as an airline employee. This is not as easily accomplished, either my exit or their staying behind, as might be imagined. The attendant has us wait in line for more than two hours, filling out each person's new flight slip by hand, tracing and retracing the numbers, reading it over again. When I finally get up to him two hours later—and there had been only two people in front of me—I get a whiff of his breath; I guess he is drunk.

Somehow he manages to fill out my papers in time for me to leave the terminal and get over to USAir. Just before I leave, I hear Joe explode in the line. Now it is his turn to act out; he shouts and fumes at the slow, drunken attendant. I wave good-bye from the escalator, ascend, get back on the monorail for the other side of the terminal, and am gone.

Gradually, after reserving a seat on the USAir flight and then getting a bit of lunch, I let the voices of my family slide off me. Those voices are heavy with guilt and shame and our childhoods; once I shed them, it is like taking off an enormous coat of mail, like shedding a raccoon coat in the beginning of spring. I bite into a Delicious apple, sip tepid coffee, eat a tasteless bagel, and revel in the solitude of the crowded terminal. But then, almost like an echo, perhaps more like an afterthought, I hear that familiar voice again: it is Tommy. At first I imagine that it is a kind of auditory hallucination, part of the stress of grieving for my father, yet it sounds too real, too near, too obviously a part of the terminal. When I look up, there they are, not all of them, but Joe and Tom, who also managed to get on the flight.

After I board the flight, the time ticks off, and I don't see either Joe or Tom come on. Maybe Tom freaked getting on the plane. Maybe he went off the deep end in the terminal. Finally Joe boards, looking weary and beat, Tom behind him dragging his bags. It turns out that Tom had gotten misplaced once again. He went off to the men's room and did not come back. He probably got into a conversation with a stranger, lingered, and then couldn't remember where we were.

Tom has the seat next to me, and the flight, unlike the one down, is crowded. He is tense, so I suggest reading. Then I think I might try a test. I ask him to read a poem by William Carlos Williams, the simple, short one about plums in the icebox. I think that perhaps he will have trouble reading the poem. Immediately he senses a trap.

"I can read all right," he says.

"Just read it," I tell him.

He does. The reading is without hesitation, direct and even intelligent. So I'm wrong about that part of his problem. Maybe, like all of us, he only needs to give his brain and body a rest from the booze. That might be all the confusion he has, though I suspect something more profound, deep-rooted, and sinister. He does promise to be open to taking medication—I think he may need it—and he is open to one of us finding him some kind of long-term therapeutic arrangement where he might work on rudimentary social skills. But he doesn't promise anything more than that. He doesn't even say he will stop drinking, and I suspect that he might have a pop as soon as he has the first opportunity, maybe in a few weeks when he gets out of this particular rehab.

When we land at LaGuardia instead of Kennedy, it is late in the evening, and I tell my brothers, since I have only the bag on my shoulder, that I am going to head on. My home in uptown Manhattan is only about fifteen to twenty minutes away at this time of night, so I will slip out of the airport and finally get that quiet I have missed for five days. Joe and Tom would take an airport car out to Long Island, no doubt at Joe's expense. I say good-bye and leave them in the terminal, Tom's interminable voice receding into the aluminum and glass, the airport rugs and the footfalls of other passengers.

As the taxi goes over the Triboro Bridge, I catch sight of the Manhattan skyline on the left, and I smell the exhaust fumes through the open window. I am back home. In fact, it is this city, I think, which is the common thread I had with my father, and maybe nothing else. I imagine that he would still be alive if, instead of moving to Florida, he and my mother had only vacationed in Florida for a few weeks a year. He'd still be alive, I think, and probably still have his brains, because he would have walked more, putting off the strokes for another day. He would have been an older person among familiar things—the Statue of Liberty, the Empire State Building, the bridges and tunnels, the Yellow cabs, subways, mass-transit buses, Shea and Yankee stadiums, even Coney Island and the Rockaways, Brooklyn Heights and Carroll Gardens, the waterfront, the docks, the piers. More important, he would have had other people who shared his outlook on life in that special way that New Yorkers have—attitude and grace, meanness and hidden kindness, crime and compassion. When he wanted to reminisce, people wouldn't have wondered what he was talking about. He would have been part of a community, and that was one of the most important parts of his identity: being a New Yorker.

Instead, my father died brainless, incompetent, incontinent, isolated and alone amid palms and alligators, geckos and floral shirts. He died in a place that was as familiar to his primitive Brooklyn mind as a foreign planet. He was gone. He is gone. He will be gone forever.

I wonder why we all, my brothers and sisters and I, were born. What purpose do I have? What is my mission in life? Why am I this man's son? Am I just like him or do I have a bit of my own humanity, something different about me that makes me unique? True, I am many people, many things to other people: a father and a lover, a husband and writer. But I am also this man's son, one of his prodigal sons come home for his funeral. Now that it is over, and unlike the biblical story in which the son stays home, I leave once again. I come back to my own world to be part of the flow, if not of the commerce then of the intellectual property, the imaginative landscape of the city.

I had returned to the world of my own obsessions and was no longer protected by that earlier generation. Now nothing separated me from eternity: I was on the front lines; I was out of the trenches and marching toward the tree line. This was it. I no longer hated my father; I even felt a tinge of sorrow as I reentered our city. More important, my family, which had been atomized when I was a child, was back. I had a kid brother, a mother, sisters, other brothers, a long continuity—all of us fighting uphill against our addictions, bad attitudes, grandiosity, and childishness. I thought about getting back into the rhythm of my life. So long, Chief.

About the Author

Michael Gregory Stephens, poet, playwright, novelist, and award-winning essayist, lives in Cambridge, Massachusetts, and is a writer-in-residence at Emerson College. Winner of the Associated Writing Programs Award for Creative Nonfiction, Stephens's many published works include the novels *The Brooklyn Book of the Dead* and *Season at Coole,* the memoir *Lost in Seoul and Other Discoveries on the Korean Peninsula, Green Dreams: Essays Under the Influence of the Irish,* a play entitled *Our Father,* and *After Asia,* a collection of poetry.

Hazelden Information and Educational Services is a division of the Hazelden Foundation, a not-for-profit organization. Since 1949, Hazelden has been a leader in promoting the dignity and treatment of people afflicted with the disease of chemical dependency.

The mission of the foundation is to improve the quality of life for individuals, families, and communities by providing a national continuum of information, education, and recovery services that are widely accessible; to advance the field through research and training; and to improve our quality and effectiveness through continuous improvement and innovation.

Stemming from that, the mission of this division is to provide quality information and support to people wherever they may be in their personal journey—from education and early intervention, through treatment and recovery, to personal and spiritual growth.

Although our treatment programs do not necessarily use everything Hazelden publishes, our bibliotherapeutic materials support our mission and the Twelve Step philosophy upon which it is based. We encourage your comments and feedback.

The headquarters of the Hazelden Foundation is in Center City, Minnesota. Additional treatment facilities are located in Chicago, Illinois; New York, New York; Plymouth, Minnesota; St. Paul, Minnesota; and West Palm Beach, Florida. At these sites, we provide a continuum of care for men and women of all ages. Our Plymouth facility is designed specifically for youth and families.

For more information on Hazelden, please call **1-800-257-7800**. Or you may access our World Wide Web site on the Internet at **www.hazelden.org**.

This book was set in Adobe Garamond, Snell Roundhand, and Trajan typefaces.